EDUCATING CHILDREN

CLASSICAL ADVICE FOR MODERN TIMES

EDUCATING CHILDREN

CLASSICAL ADVICE FOR MODERN TIMES

Imam Muhammad bin Ahmed al-Ramli's Riyadatul Sibyan
Translation and Commentary by Abdul Aziz Ahmed

BEACON BOOKS

Published in the UK by Beacon Books and Media Ltd
Earl Business Centre, Dowry Street, Oldham, OL8 2PF, UK.

Previously published in 2013 by Kitaba (Islamic Texts for the Blind) and Dar al-Turath al-Islami.

www.beaconbooks.net

ISBN 978-1-915025-89-0 Paperback
ISBN 978-1-915025-90-6 Hardback
ISBN 978-1-915025-91-3 Ebook

Cataloging-in-Publication record for this book is available from the British Library.

Cover design by Raees Mahmood Khan

Contents

بِسْمِ اللَّهِ الرَّحْمَنِ الرَّحِيمِ

In the name of Allah, Most Gracious, Most Merciful

TRANSLATOR'S INTRODUCTION

وَأَمَّا بِنِعْمَةِ رَبِّكَ فَحَدِّثْ

But the bounty of your Lord – rehearse and proclaim

All praise and thanks are due to Allāh who blessed His servants with innumerable opportunities, bounties and privileges. If I were to attempt to enumerate and proclaim the bounties Allāh granted me, among the first would be my two healthy children. I would also recall the opportunities He provided for me to study. I attended the classes of great men like al-Ḥabīb Aḥmed Mashūr al-Ḥaddād, al-Ḥabīb 'Abdul Qādir al-Saqqaf and al-Sayyid Muḥammad bin 'Alawi al-Mālikī. I received the care and attention of my loving parents, my teachers and spiritual guides including al-Ḥabīb 'Abdul Raḥmān al-Khitāmy. Their guidance and direction were blessings, the reality of which only began to become clear once they departed from this world, leaving us to deal with overwhelming emptiness and yearning.

My 'rehearsing and proclaiming' of these bounties is partly in response to the above mentioned verse, but also because they are directly relevant to the commentary and translation you have before you. *Riyāḍatul Ṣibyān* is a classical Arabic text on educating children. As a teacher trained in the West, I would not have had access to this book without the great men I have mentioned. I was born in Nottingham in the United Kingdom and spent the vast majority of my life in the Western world where my children were born and brought up. The influences of traditional Islamic teaching and Western education have undoubtedly shaped the way I brought up my own children. As they move on through adulthood, I can now reflect on this text in a way I could not have done without the experiences of my own development under the influences of my parents and teachers, the valuable pedagogical tradition I experienced through my studies, the twenty-five years of teaching learners of various ages from nursery children to adults, and witnessing my own children grow and thrive.

The book includes some traditional commentary as well as personal reflection. To ensure the reader does not confuse my personal opinions with classical and well-established theological positions, I have structured each section so that it contains four elements. First, is the original Arabic text with an English translation. After the translation, there is a commentary showing the traditional understanding of the classical scholars of Islam. The third section has been entitled 'reflections' and is my own personal interpretation. It is hoped that this complements, and does not contradict, traditional understanding and orthodox principles. The final section contains discussion questions that I have used in training sessions. The questions prompted closer examination of the text and an opportunity to relate the text to issues facing parents and teachers in a modern context. The discussion was further developed using a Facebook forum.

For the 'traditional' commentary, I have relied heavily on *Simt al-'Uqyān* by 'Abdullāh bin Aḥmed Bā Saudān and the chapter in al-Ghazālī's *Iḥyā 'Ulūm al-Dīn* on which the poem was based and after which it was titled. T. J. Winter has produced a superb translation of this in his book *Al-Ghazālī on Disciplining the Soul*. For definitions and in trying to get the best translation of a particular word, I have used the classical lexical reference works including *Lisān al-'Arab* and *Mukhtār al-Ṣiḥāḥ* as well as traditional commentaries of *ḥadīth*, Prophetic tradition, in which the words are used. Wherever a *ḥadīth* is quoted, I have tried to use classical commentaries to obtain the most well-established explanation and most accurate translation. The primary commentaries used in this work are by Imām al-Nawawī, Ibn Ḥajar and 'Abdul Ra'ūf al-Munāwī.

The psychological tradition that most influences my thinking is that of Vygotsky and Bruner. I am happy to work in an environment where the rights and protection of the child are of paramount importance, and where equality and inclusion are key principles. I hope these influences have enhanced and not corrupted my exposure to classical Islamic scholarship. I do not expect the reader to accept all that I have written here or to agree with me. However, I pray that each reader gains some benefit from this book and that it makes us all think about how we educate our children. I ask Allāh to forgive my mistakes and for the reader to overlook any shortcomings and faults they find in this book. *Āmīn.*

Imām Muḥammad bin Aḥmed al-Ramlī

Imām al-Ramlī is known by many titles including Shamsuddīn, the Sun of the Religion, the Small Shāfi, Shaykh al-Islām, Imām al-Ḥaramayn, Imām of the Two Sacred Mosques and Shaykh of the Egyptians.

He was born in Egypt in a village called al-Ramla near Manūfiya, North West of Cairo in Jumādī al-Awwal in 919 H (July 1513 CE). He grew up under the keen eye of his father and teacher, Imām Aḥmed Shihābuddīn al-Ramlī. His father was the main source of scholarship for the region and all contemporary Egyptian scholars would refer to him. Most had been taught directly by him. For this reason, his father said of his son that he left him without need of any other teacher except in rare circumstances. As a young child, he attended the lessons of his father's teacher, Imām Zakariyya al-Anṣārī for blessings as he was too young to benefit from the actual content. Among the teachers he shared with his father was Burhānuddīn al-Qudsī who studied under Imām Ibn Ḥajar al-ʿAsqalānī. Al-Shaʿrānī said of the son, 'I kept company with him from the time I would carry him on my shoulders as a child until now [that is the time of writing his biographical work *al-Ṭabaqāt al-Wusṭa*] and I never saw anything reprehensible. He did not used to play with children; rather he grew up in righteousness, shelter, protection of his limbs and in purity.'[1]

After his father's death, Shamsuddīn took over his father's class and most of his father's students, including great scholars like Imām al-Shaʿrānī. He would teach all the major Islamic sciences including *ḥadīth*, exegesis, jurisprudence, grammar, logic and rhetoric. He took up the role of Muftī, established several schools, and authored many books including collections of his father's legal opinions and commentaries on classical texts from the Shāfi school of jurisprudence. His most famous text was *Nihāyatul Muḥtāj Sharḥ al-Minhāj*. He died in Jumādī al-Awwal 1004 H, January 1596 CE.

In the Islamic tradition, scholars write short texts known as *mutūn*, which are then expounded by later generations. These commentaries are called *shurūḥ* (singular *sharḥ*). Some of these *mutūn* or basic texts have been put into poetry known as *nazam*. These poems are easier to memorise and study. These rhyming versions are sometimes commented upon by other scholars. In this way, the words of earlier generations are preserved, but the ideas are explained in new contexts by different scholars.

This is what you have before you. The *nazam* is a rhyming version of one of the books of Imām al-Ghazālī which appears in his collection entitled *Iḥyā 'Ulūm al-Dīn*, the Revival of the Religious Sciences. The *Iḥyā* contains 'forty books', one of which is called *Riyāḍatul Nafs*, Disciplining the Self. This book has a section on educating children called *Riyāḍatul Ṣibyān*. There are several commentaries on al-Ramlī's poem but the most famous, and the one used for this book, is that of the Yemeni scholar 'Abdullāh Bā Saudān.

'Abdullāh Bā Saudān and His Commentary

'Abdullāh bin Aḥmed Bā Saudān was one of Ḥadramaut's most famous scholars. He was born in 1187 H (1773 CE) in the Do'ān Valley which is also known as the Valley of the Jurists because it has produced so many scholars. One of his ancestors lived in a village named Ghayl Saudān before moving to Do'ān. After the migration, his descendants became known as Bā Saudān, meaning children of Saudān. 'Abdullāh studied the Quran and his initial Islamic studies in the town of Khuraiba. He later went with his teacher, 'Umar bin 'Abdul Raḥmān al-Bār, to the main towns of Ḥadramaut for further studies and visits to its main scholars.

He continued visiting Ḥadramaut with his shaykh until 1212 H, when he travelled to Makka for pilgrimage. Tragically for 'Abdullāh, his shaykh passed away on the way to the Hajj. 'Abdullāh Bā Saudān had many other prominent teachers including Aḥmed bin Ḥasan bin 'Abdullāh al-Ḥaddād, 'Umar bin Zayn bin Sumait and Ṭāhir bin Ḥussain bin Ṭāhir.

He had many great students including Ṭāhir bin 'Umar al-Ḥaddād, Ṣāliḥ bin 'Abdullāh al-Aṭṭās and 'Aidarūs bin 'Umar al-Ḥabashī.

'Abdullāh Bā Saudān wrote several books, including a commentary on the basic Islamic primer by Aḥmed bin Zayn al-Ḥabashī entitled *Anwār al-Lāmi'a wa Tatimātu Wāsia' 'alā Risālatul Jāmia'* and a book on the laws of marriage entitled *al-Ifsāḥ 'an aḥkām al-Nikāḥ*. He also produced a commentary on the litany of Imām al-Ḥaddād called *Dhakhīratul Ma'ād bī Sharḥ Rāṭib al-Ḥaddād*. He died shortly before dawn on the 7th of Jumādū al-Ūla 1266 H (20th April 1850).

Riyādatul Ṣibyān: 'Training Boys or Educating Children'?

Riyāḍa means 'physical training, domestication (of an animal), sport, mathematics, relaxation or spiritual exercise.' The origin of the word *riyāḍa* is 'a piece of land that has been cultivated.' A quality that underlies the concept of 'training, mathematics, and spiritual exercises' is that they all require effort and exertion in a repetitive fashion until such a time that the skill concerned is mastered. A garden does not become a *riyāḍa* except through hard work. An athlete excels after rigorous training. Mathematics is mastered by repeating drills and exercises. A spiritual novice rises in rank based on his spiritual exercises.

An important term, used frequently in this commentary and related to *riyāḍa*, is the word *tarbiyya*, development. It is used for both gardening and nurturing young children. The imagery of the two words *riyāḍa* and *tarbiyya* in their gardening context are relevant to my choice of title. Education is more than just training. It is more than just nurturing. I hope that through the commentary and reflection the reader will begin to understand, and perhaps appreciate, the choice of title. It is important because it sets the tone for the approach adopted in the commentary and reflection.

Ṣibyān is the plural of *ṣabiy*, which means boy. A literal translation of the title might be 'training boys' and some have suggested I should have taken a literal approach in this book. It is clear that the address is very much to the father about how he should develop 'manly' qualities in his son. However, I have adopted the more general title *Educating Children* as it is clear that the lessons are applicable to both genders, and that grammatically 'boys' can imply 'boys and girls'.

May Allāh grant success to the reader, producers and translator of this work. For only through Him is there enabling ability.

Endnotes

1 Muḥammad bin Aḥmed al-Ramlī, "Publisher's foreword", in *Fawā'id al-Mardiyya: Sharḥ Mukhtaṣar al-Muqaddimatul Ḥardrāmiyya*, (Jeddah: Alam al-Ma'rūf, 1999).

1

AUTHOR'S FOREWORD: PART ONE

In the name of Allāh, Most Gracious, Most Merciful

اَلْحَمْدُ لِلّٰهِ وَلِيِّ الْحَمْدِ - مُوَفِّقِ الْخَلْقِ لِكُلِّ رُشْدِ

عَلَى الَّذِي بِهِ عَلَيْنَا أَنْعَمَا - حَمْدًا يَعُمُّ الأَرْضَ وَالسَّمَا

ثُمَّ الصَّلَاةُ بَعْدَ مَا قُلْنَا بِهِ - عَلَى النَّبِي وَآلِهِ وَصَحْبِهِ

وَبَعْدُ : فَالتَّأْدِيبُ لِلصِّبْيَانِ - مِنْ أَوَّلِ النَّشْوِ أَتَمُّ الشَّانِ

وَقَدْ بِذَاكَ صَرَّحَ الْغَزَالِي - بَحْرُ الْعُلُومِ صَادِقُ الْمَقَالِ

وَحَثَّ فِي [إِحْيَا عُلُومِ الدِّينِ] - عَلَى قِيَامِ الأَهْلِ بِالْبَنِينِ

All praise is to the One who deserves all praise
The One who makes humankind amenable to guidance
For what He has bestowed upon us
A praise that encompasses the earth and the sky

And after what we have said comes salutations
Upon the Prophet and his family and Companions
And following on – (know that) the education of children
From the initial stages is a great affair

And certainly al-Ghazālī has made that clear
(And he is) an ocean of knowledge, true in his advice
He encouraged in Iḥyā Ulūm al-Dīn
The responsibility of parents towards their children

Commentary

All praise is to the One who deserves all praise, the One who makes humankind amenable to guidance, for what He has bestowed upon us, a praise that encompasses the earth and the sky.

Imām al-Ramlī begins in the traditional manner, starting in the name of Allāh and then praising Him. Allāh is deserving of *all* praise but here special praise is singled out for that which 'He has bestowed upon us,' meaning our existence and guidance to Islam. The author then sends salutations and prayers upon the one who brought that guidance, the Holy Prophet Muḥammad, and prays for the Prophet's family and Companions.

Know that the education (ta'dīb) of children from the initial stages is a great affair.

Ta'dīb is the process of giving someone *adab*, which is defined as 'putting something in its correct place'. In this sense, it is used for training as in the Prophetic statement: 'Three things are not considered time-wasting – training a horse (*ta'dīb al-fars*), playing with the family and shooting arrows (for practice).'[1] The horse, after '*ta'dīb*', is no longer 'wild' and has lost some of its lower impulses. It has been 'trained' or 'cultured.'

The roots of the word, */a-da-ba/*, which means 'to be invited to a wedding feast.' It is connected to the word *ma'daba*, banquet. At the feast, the eating utensils and seating arrangements should all be in specific places. This act of being precise in arrangements is the process of *adab*. Those who attend the feast should show the correct eating and dress etiquette. As a result, *adab* is more generally understood to mean 'placing something in its correct place' or 'giving someone or something its correct due' so that we have *adab* to our parents, *adab* towards the Quran, the *adab* of eating, and so on. The one who knows these etiquettes and implements them is called *adīb*. The translation of *adīb* is usually polite, cultured and courteous. It is also used for a man of letters, who excels in penmanship and grammar. We can see that *adab* in a general sense means knowing one's place and the place of others.

Sayyid Muḥammad Naquīb al-Aṭṭās said: 'The fundamental element inherent in the concept of education in Islam is the inculcation of *adab* (*ta'dīb*), for it is *adab* in the all-inclusive sense I mean, as encompassing the spiritual and material life of a man, that instils the quality of goodness sought after.'[2] These spiritual and societal dimensions of *adab* have their roots in the Quran, and in this sense, the adopting of culture, the training of the lower self, and learning of appropriate behaviour are all drawn from the Quran and the behaviour of the Prophet, upon him be peace. He said: 'My Lord gave me *adab* and excelled in the giving of my *adab*.'[3] And he, upon him be peace, said: 'The Quran is Allāh's banquet (*ma'daba*).'[4]

The two concepts are directly connected. The Prophet's character was described by his wife, 'Āisha, may Allāh be pleased with her, when she said: 'His character was that of the Quran.'[5] The Quran is the 'banquet' from which we feast until our inner beings overflow with its meanings and blessings, and then become apparent through our character. When it flows from us, we will have a portion of the Prophetic character which he received directly, without schooling from His Creator. Through the process of 'feasting' on the Quran and through the guidance which he, upon whom be peace, received directly from Allāh, we will understand the behaviour appropriate to each situation. We will show inner and outer etiquette to our Creator, ourselves, our families, and all of creation. For this reason, inculcating *adab* is described in the poem as 'a great affair.'

The phrase 'from the initial stages', according to Bā Saudān, refers to the point where a child can distinguish between right and wrong. This should be understood in the context of the *ḥadīth* in which the Prophet, upon him be peace, is reported to have said: 'Choose well for your embryos for surely genes will be transferred.'[6] The literal translation would be 'surely the umbilical cord transmits' implying that character traits are inherited by the child from the mother. This is why the 'initial stages' of parenting begin when one chooses a spouse. It is for this reason that the Prophet, upon him be peace, said: 'Be careful of *al-ḥaḍara al-dimn* [a beautiful green shrub]!'[7] The Companions asked: 'What are the *al-ḥaḍara al-dimn*?' 'Beautiful women of low origin,' he, upon him be peace, replied. The author says it is a 'great affair' meaning it is 'important and a compulsion.' The Exalted commands:

يَا أَيُّهَا الَّذِينَ آمَنُوا قُوا أَنفُسَكُمْ وَأَهْلِيكُمْ نَارًا وَقُودُهَا النَّاسُ وَالْحِجَارَةُ عَلَيْهَا مَلَائِكَةٌ غِلَاظٌ شِدَادٌ لَا يَعْصُونَ اللَّهَ مَا أَمَرَهُمْ وَيَفْعَلُونَ مَا يُؤْمَرُونَ

O ye who believe! Save yourselves and your families from a Fire whose fuel is Men and Stones, over which are (appointed) angels stern (and) severe, who flinch not (from executing) the Commands they receive from Allāh, but do (precisely) what they are commanded. (al-Taḥrīm 66:6)

And certainly al-Ghazālī has made that clear.

The poet states that this text is based largely on the work of Imām Abū Ḥāmid al-Ghazālī. He describes him as *ṣādiq al-maqāl* which literally means 'truthful in his words' but implies he was 'sincere in his advice and guidance.' *Ṣādiq* is also a reference to his spiritual status. The highest spiritual status a non-Prophet can reach is that of *siddīqiyyatul kubrā*.

Imām al-Ghazālī was born in the Central Asian town of Ṭūs in 1058 CE. He became a renowned jurist and theologian before facing a spiritual crisis after which he took a break from public life. On his return to public scholarship and writing, he produced his most important work *Iḥyā ʿUlūm al-Dīn*, The Revival of the Religious Sciences. It discusses the inner and outer aspects of the religion in a practical manner. The *Iḥyā* contains forty books, one of which is called *Disciplining the Self* (*Riyāḍatul Nafs*). One of the sections in the book is entitled *Riyāḍatul Ṣibyān* which is what Imām al-Ramlī based this poem upon.

Imām al-Ghazālī died in Ṭūs in 1111 CE (505 H). He was described by Horten as 'the greatest ethical thinker of Islam.'[8]

Reflection

What is education?

There are several terms for education in Arabic. They include *ta'dīb*, which is discussed above, *taʿlīm* or *tadrīs*, which both mean 'teaching' or 'giving of knowledge' and *tarbiyya* which implies 'development' or 'growth'.

Reflecting on the commentary above, two important things come to mind. Aṭṭās links the concept of *adab* to justice. In Arabic, the opposite of justice is *ẓulm*, which is defined as 'placing something in its improper place'. For this reason, one may do injustice to others by denying them their rights, but more importantly one may do injustice to oneself. One who has wronged himself cannot really be balanced in his relationships with others. This contains an important lesson for parents and educators. Being in balance with oneself or having *adab* towards oneself means understanding what the self is. Human nature is connected to the Divine Covenant where Allāh asked us: 'Am I not your Lord?'[9] Part of us yearns for that Divine Discourse and recognition of His Lordship and our slavehood. Part of us is driven by the lower ego described in the Quran as *al-nafs al-amāra*, which drives us to animalistic passion and pursuit of personal pleasure. When the self that yearns for the Divine overcomes the lower animalistic self, the person has *adab* with himself. This is the meaning of *ta'dīb*. We, as parents and teachers, need to work on our own *ta'dīb*, self discipline, and likewise ensure that when we deal with children we show justice and not *ẓulm*. Children understand justice and injustice because part of them is closer to the primordial state known as *fiṭra* and therefore it is our *ẓulm* that corrupts their state, and our *adab* that develops *adab* within them. This, for me, is the meaning of education.

Linguistically, the term *tarbiyya* has three meanings. It means 'increase' and 'growing up' and 'to make right'. For this reason, al-Qurṭubī defines it as 'the reaching of something to a state of perfection, step by step.'[10] Drawing on the linguistic definition, we can see that *tarbiyya* implies preservation of the child's natural state (*fiṭra*), providing the conditions for growth and ensuring this growth leads to what is best for the child.

The concept of *tarbiyya* is very important in my mind. I am probably influenced by the opinion of Rousseau that 'plants are fashioned by cultivation, man by education.'[11] This implies that education is the process of nurturing a child into becoming an adult. It is the same word used for gardening. The *tarbiyya* of plants requires one to choose the right soil, to water and feed the seedling and strengthen and support the growing plant. By doing this correctly and with God's enabling power (*tawfiq*), you will see the plant flourish, flower and fruit. Likewise, caring for a child and meeting his or her spiritual needs is the essence of education and leads to the *murabbiy*, teacher, seeing the child develop into a thriving and happy adult.

When I was living in Saudi Arabia, someone was intrigued as to what an Englishman dressed in Arab clothes and speaking Arabic was doing in Jeddah. I explained that I was a teacher and his face lit up (probably thinking I could tutor his children). When he asked what subject I taught, I told him I was a primary school teacher. In near disgust, he said '*ah, bass murabbiy*', meaning 'oh just a child carer'. His tone of voice questioned my manhood and intelligence. At the time, I felt offended, but on reflecting upon it I realise that it was quite a compliment to be called 'a carer'. Caring is not gender specific. The Prophet, upon him be peace, is described in the Quran as *ra'ūf* and *raḥīm* meaning concerned for others and merciful. These two qualities are at the core of being a carer, and 'carer' would be an apt description of the Prophet, upon him be peace. It was not until very recently that I heard the term used again about my role. During a presentation about our last trip to Makka, the presenter pointed out a photo of me with a wheelchair user and a blind brother, and the caption read 'Ricardo, Balal and their carer'. Until then, I had not thought of myself as a carer, but now I will take the term as a badge of honour.

Discussion

Tarbiyya ***is the nurturing of a child or a plant. What things does a child require to thrive?***

Children and young people need:

- Basic health requirements to be met, such as good diet, sleep, active hobbies, etc.
- Parents who respect and offer compliments to each other, and who laugh and speak gently to each other
- Unconditional acceptance and love from their parents or guardians
- Adults and role models who have clear values and consistently act according to them
- Praise when they do things well, and explanation in child-friendly language when they do not
- Structure and routines
- Teaching in a manner that is appropriate to their learning style
- Opportunities and space to learn from their mistakes

Mariam, Educational Psychologist, Copenhagen

'Children's development is shaped by many influences, including genetic makeup, early interactions with parents or other caregivers, socioeconomic factors, and early childhood experiences in the family, at school, and in the community. Children need love and positive regard from trusted family members and other adults. They thrive on affection and loving attention and encouragement. It is also important to have boundaries set concerning their behaviour.

Children should be given the opportunity to explore the arts, be exposed to a wide variety of educational and cultural activities, and learn manual skills, so that they can find their gifts.

Children need a safe neighbourhood in which to live and play. Neighbourhoods have a lot of influence on whether or not children thrive.'

Eva, Parent, Bristol

Endnotes

1 Related by Abū Dawūd, *ḥadīth* number 2513.

2 Sayyid Muḥammad Naquīb al-Aṭṭās, *Aims and Objectives of Islamic Education* (Jeddah: Hodder and Stoughton, 1977), 1.

3 Related by al-Sam'ānī on the authority of Ibn Mas'ūd and considered to be authentic (*ṣaḥīḥ*) by al-Suyūṭī.

4 Related by al-Ḥākim on the authority of Ibn Mas'ūd.

5 Related by Muslim, *ḥadīth* number 746.

6 Related by Ibn Mājah on the authority of 'Āisha.

7 Related by al-Darquṭunī and al-Daylamī on the authority of Abū Sa'īd.

8 M. Horten, *Die Philosophie des Islamin ihren Beziehungen sudden philosophischen Weltanschauungen des westlichen Orients* (Munich, 1924), 24.

9 Al-A'rāf, 7:172.

10 Abu 'Abdullāh Muḥammad Aḥmed al-Ansari al-Qurṭubī, "Commentary on the opening chapter of the Quran", in *Anwār al-Tanzīl wa Asrār al-Tawīl*, (Beirut: Dar al-Kuṭub, 1988).

11 Jean-Jacques Rousseau, *Emile*, trans. Barbara Foxley (London: Everyman, 1993), 6.

2

AUTHOR'S FOREWORD: PART TWO

لأَنَّ تَأْدِيبَ الصَّبِي فِي صِغَرِهْ - زِيَادَةٌ لِحَظِّهِ فِي كِبَرِهْ

يَنَالُ فِي ذَاكَ الْحُظُوظَ الْوَافِرَهْ - وَرَاحَةَ الدُّنْيَا وَخَيْرَ الآخِرَهْ

فَيَنْبَغِي لِكُلِّ جَدٍّ وَأَبِ - وَقَيِّمِ الْحَاكِمِ تَأْدِيبُ الصَّبِي

لأَنَّهُ أَمَانَةٌ عِنْدَهُمُ - وَقَلْبُهُ يَقْبَلُ تَأْدِيبَهُمُ

وَتَنْهَرُ الأُمُّ وَلَدَهَا بِالأَبِ - زَجْراً لَهُ عَنِ الْخَنَا وَاللَّعِبِ

إِذْ قَلْبُهُ كَالشَّمْعَةِ الْمَقْصُورَهْ - مُجَوْهَرٌ يَقْبَلُ كُلَّ صُورَهْ

فَيَنْبَغِي لَهُمْ بِأَنْ يُعَوِّدُوا - أَوْلَادَهُمْ فِعْلَ التُّقَى لِيُسْعَدُوا

The upbringing of a child in the early years
Will increase his portion in the later years
And in that he will gain, in abundance, good fortune,
Peace in this world and the goodness of the Next

Therefore educating the child is a must for every grandfather,
Father and every one given responsibility
For he is a trust granted to them
And his heart is open to their education

The mother should caution her child with the father
Protecting him from inequity and folly
His heart is like a pure candle
Able to adopt any form

And so it is necessary that they habituate
Their children to doing righteous deeds so they attain felicity

Commentary

The upbringing of a child in the early years will increase his portion in the later years.

The phrase *fī sighrihī* literally means 'when he is small'. In the words of Bā Saudān, it refers to 'the state in which he is able to accept [such education]. It is writing on the clean slate of his heart.'[1]

The wife of one of our teachers said that this stage is like preparing dough. You can mix it in whichever way you wish and the product will be clear once it has risen. She also said a child at this stage is like a young tree that can be blown in the wind. As it grows, it becomes thick and immoveable.

The verse suggests that the benefits of education will be seen later in life and in the Hereafter. Al-Ghazālī says about the child in the early years: 'If it is habituated to and instructed in goodness then this will be its practice when it grows up, and it will attain to felicity in this world and the next; its parents too, and all its teachers and preceptors will share in its reward.'[2] An alternative understanding of this verse is that if a child learns *adab*, good manners, as a child, he or she will earn the respect of others when he or she is older.

The benefits of education are abundant. The author uses the word *al-ḥuẓūẓ*, 'portions' in the plural in Arabic to emphasise the multitude of blessings that are obtained through attaining good manners and education. *Wāfira* implies 'perfect' or 'complete'. The translation might read 'he attains perfect portions and peace, in this world and the next' but we have opted for the above translation as it conveys the meaning in a simpler manner.

The 'peace of this world' is the ability to access knowledge, to enjoy research and the discovery of the intricacies of words and concepts. Education provides us with the opportunity to worship correctly and live our lives in a state of good physical, mental and spiritual health.

Therefore educating the child is a must for every grandfather, father and everyone given responsibility.

The first part of this verse outlines the order of responsibility in Islam. The parents are responsible for the child. If they are incapable or have passed away, the duty is passed onto the grandparents and then to the wider community. The wider community are encouraged to foster and adopt orphans. The Messenger, upon him be peace, said: 'The best home among the Muslims is one in which there is an orphan who is treated well.'[3] It is reported that once an orphan was being teased for having no father, to which he replied, 'You have one father, but everyone's father is my father.' This is the spirit encouraged by the Prophet and the early communities. He, upon him be peace, said: 'Whoever places his hand on the head of an orphan showing mercy will receive reward for every hair he passes over.'[4]

The parents, grandparents and those responsible for the child should take great care of their own behaviour in front of the children, and foster a good relationship with the child as everything they do will affect the child's life. Al-Ghazālī says: 'A child is a trust in the care of the parents, for his heart is a precious uncut jewel devoid of any form or carving, which will accept being cut into any shape, and will be disposed according to the guidance it receives from others.'[5]

The mother should caution her child with the father.

Al-Ghazālī says: 'The mother, when reproving him, should frighten him by [threatening to mention the matter to] his father.'[6]

Al-Ḥabīb Ḥusayn Balfaqīh points out that the success of the *tarbiyya* of the child is dependent on the perception the child has of his parents. The father has a responsibility to make sure that he is always seen as upright and act as a role model whom the child is in awe of. He suggests that if, for example, the father has the bad habit of smoking he should do so far from the eyes of the child so that his image as a good role model is not damaged.

Reflection

What are the roles of the mother and father?

I like the examples offered by al-Ḥabīb Ḥusayn. Many might interpret these lines as a suggestion that the father should be seen as a terrifying tyrant who threatens the child. This is far from reality. Imām al-Ḥaddād says: 'It has been narrated that a man will be counted among the tyrants – although he had no responsibilities in this world other than his family, yet, he wronged them and acted unjustly towards them.'[7]

Any reading of the biography of the Prophet, upon him be peace, should leave the reader with no doubt that he was the model father. He, upon him be peace, used to joke more with his family than his Companions. The awe that his children, Companions and family had was based on the fear of upsetting him or of losing that love and gentleness. He was kind, merciful, and loving but also fair and just. Being kind and merciful does not contradict the verse:

الرِّجَالُ قَوَّامُونَ عَلَى النِّسَاءِ بِمَا فَضَّلَ اللّٰهُ بَعْضَهُمْ عَلَى بَعْضٍ
وَبِمَا أَنفَقُواْ مِنْ أَمْوَالِهِمْ

Men shall take full care of women with the bounties which God has bestowed more abundantly on the former than on the latter and with what they may spend out of their possessions. (al-Nisā 4:34)

There are several ways of translating the concept mentioned in this verse, where men are described as *qawwāmun* over women. I have used Muḥammad Asad's translation as I feel statements like 'men are in charge of women' and 'men are protectors and maintainers of women' may be misleading.

The father is described as *qawwām*, which means guardian or caretaker over the whole family, including the mother. The word also implies 'justness' and 'proportion'. Al-Qurṭubī in his commentary says the verse describes the role of men in the family: 'They maintain their living expenses' and al-Baghawī says men are 'responsible for establishing what is best for them.' There are unchangeable legal responsibilities implied in these verses. According to Islamic law, men will always have legal duties and responsibilities which women do not. A woman who works is not responsible for spending on her husband and children. If she does choose to spend upon her family, as was the case with the Prophet's wife Khadīja, may Allāh be pleased with her, she does so out of kindness and not as an obligation or duty. The legal duty remains upon the husband and should be carried out with love and fairness. He is expected to fulfil his duties and his wife is expected to show him love and respect. These have been the traditional roles in Muslim societies, and historically in the West. The father was the provider and the mother a carer. However, for those living in the West, the traditional family structure has become increasingly unclear. Women are more likely to be breadwinners than in the past. The role of mothers will inevitably have to develop under these changing circumstances. Among my own teachers was one who lost his job shortly before the birth of his daughter. For most of her early years, he took care of her at home, while his wife continued to work. He remained (in my view) *qawwām* in the full sense of the word, yet his role was far from the traditional Islamic scholar. It is impossible to say there is only one 'Islamic' model. The role of the father and mother will depend on circumstances, the nature of the father, mother and child, and on the cultural norms in which the child is growing.

The challenge of changing circumstances is in maintaining the principles set out in the Quran and the words of scholars, yet presenting role models that are relevant and sustainable in an ever-changing world. The challenge is not unique to the Muslim community. These changes affect all communities and many are questioning whether these traditional models can still work. Sue Palmer suggests: 'Part of the problem with modern child-rearing is that as women's roles in society have changed, essential knowledge has been forgotten. In the past, bringing up children was always "women's work", and through the centuries women learned a lot about their charges. Information about children's needs was passed from mother to daughter and back up by grandmothers and other "wise women" in the community. In the revolutionary change of the last few decades, much of this ancient wisdom has disappeared.' She concludes that 'gradually, however, science has confirmed that much of the ancient wisdom was true.'[8]

Discussion

Should men and women have distinct roles in bringing up children? If so, what should they be? Are there cases where they overlap?

'Yes, a child needs to be exposed to both feminine and masculine values/characteristics. However, it is not necessarily the women who need to be the feminine ones and men who need to be the masculine ones.

The thing about the mother using the father as a threat to get the child to behave lowers the authority and the child's respect for the mother.'

Group of sisters at a course in Copenhagen

'Men need to be men and women need to be women, otherwise children grow up confused.'

Ahmed Skaka, Adelaide

'Muslims with a migrant background have to change their parenting approach from how they were brought up. Parents I have interviewed worked as a team with each other.'

Aminah Mah, Researcher at University of Western Australia, Perth

'Traditional roles have changed, but have they really changed that much? Haven't assertive women and gentle men always been around? I am thinking of the stories we have heard about the Companions, and the way that, for example, the men of Makka complained about the women of Madina controlling their husbands. I agree with the fact that both men and women possess different amounts of conventionally male/female characteristics. But I personally feel that the husband/father should still have a degree of ultimate authority and the mother/wife should give him that.'

Anonymous, Facebook Page

'There are two important ingredients that are needed in parenting and they are compassion and flexibility. For example, if the mother is feeling unwell the father should be able to adapt accordingly and not continue to expect too much from their spouse. Rigid roles can lead to oppression from either parent and in my opinion it is usually the mother who is expected to take all the work regardless of the situation.'

Massarat Jan, Primary School Teacher, Birmingham

'Let them agree in the ordering of their duties as well as in their method, let the child pass from one to the other.'

Jean-Jacques Rousseau, French Philosopher

'Fathers should inspire awe, but through gentleness and kindness. The mother should "threaten the child with the father". This is the norm. But in some cases, the mother (by her nature) may be stern and strong and, as long as the father is gentle and kind, this can have a good outcome. It is when both are permissive and easy about everything or both are always harsh and strict and "crack the whip" in every situation, whether it is appropriate or not, that the environment becomes corrupted. The nature of the child is that he or she requires sternness and parameters as well as mercy and kindness.'[9]

Al-Ḥabīb 'Umar Bin Ḥafīẓ, Islamic Scholar

Endnotes

1 'Abdullāh bin Aḥmed Bā Saudān, *Simt al-'Uqyān* (Beirut: Dār al-Faqīh, 2004), 83.

2 Abū Ḥāmid Muḥammad ibn Muḥammad Al-Ghazālī, *On Disciplining the Soul and on Breaking the Two Desires*, trans. Timothy Winters (Cambridge: The Islamic Texts Society, 1995), 78.

3 Related by al-Bukhārī and considered to be authentic by al-Suyūṭī and by Ibn Mājah *ḥadīth* number 3679.

4 Related by Aḥmed on the authority of Abū 'Umāma.

5 Al-Ghazālī, *On Disciplining the Soul*, 78.

6 Ibid.

7 'Abdullāh ibn 'Alawi al-Ḥaddādi, *al-Naṣā'ih al-Dīnniyya wal Waṣāya al-Imāniyya* (Beirut: Dār al-Hāwī, 1999), 280.

8 Sue Palmer, *Detoxing Childhood: What parents need to know to raise happy successful children* (London: Orion Books, 2007), 4.

9 "Educating Children by al-Ḥabīb 'Umar", accessed May 9, 2009, http://www.daralmustafaedu.com/.

3

EARLY YEARS: SUCKLING

وَأَوَّلُ الأَشْيَا هِيَ الْحَضَانَهْ - لأَنَّهُ مَعْ أَهْلِهِ أَمَانَهْ

فَيَنْبَغِي إِرْضَاعُ كُلِّ طِفْلِ - صَالِحَةً بِقَوْلِهَا وَالْفِعْلِ

تَأْكُلْ حَلاَلاً لاَ مِنَ الْحَرَامِ - فَالطَّبْعُ قَالُوا تَابِعُ الطَّعَامِ

إِذَا خَبُثْ رَضَاعُهُ مَالَ إِلَى - فِعْلِ الْخَبِيثِ آخِراً وَأَوَّلاَ

The first of things is the nursery period (ḥaḍāna)
Because his family with him are entrusted
It is desirable that the suckling of every child
Should be from one righteous in her words and deeds

Who eats from the permitted and not the illicit
For they have said one's habits will reflect what he eats
If the suckling is filthy, he inclines towards
Filthy actions, firstly and lastly

Commentary

The first of things is the nursery period.

Linguistically, *ḥaḍāna*, means 'to keep by one's side'. During this period, the mother keeps the child close to her. It is connected to the word *ḥiḍan*, 'outstretched arms', which has connotations of hugging and welcoming. In legal language, the period of *ḥaḍāna* is the time before the child reaches the age of discrimination (*tamyīz*) and is able to distinguish between right and wrong.

His family with him are entrusted.

The child is said to be an *amāna*, trust, and has been entrusted by Allāh to his family. An *amāna* is a trust granted to someone to look after it until the rightful owner wants it back. We say 'we are from Allāh and to Him we will return' meaning that He is our owner and master. The child is entrusted to his or her parents to be looked after and cared for. The one who is given an *amāna* should have certain qualities, including trustworthiness, honour, and the ability to look after the trust with gentleness and mercy.

It is desirable that the suckling of every child should be from one righteous in her words and deeds.

Al-Ghazālī says that whoever is entrusted with the upbringing of the child should 'watch over him diligently from his earliest days, and permit none but a woman of virtue and religion to nurse and raise him; her diet should be of permitted things, for there is no blessing (*baraka*) in milk which originates in forbidden food which, should a child be nourished on it, will knead his native disposition in such a way as to incline his temperament to wrongdoing.'[1]

The verses relate to a topic discussed earlier, that it is important when considering a marriage partner to look at him or her as the potential father or mother of one's children. If the mother of your child does not eat from the permitted, the child will be brought up on the illicit. It flows in her milk and corrupts the child's nature. If the child is to be wet nursed, as was the tradition in many cultures, one should be just as careful about choosing a wet nurse.

If the suckling is filthy, he inclines towards filthy actions, firstly and lastly.

We must be careful and circumspect about deciding from whom they are suckled and where they eat. The Imām says, they are affected by what and from whom they eat. 'If the suckling is filthy, he inclines to filthy actions.'

Khabīth, filthy, according to al-Munāwi, means 'reprehensible, vile and contemptible and encompasses the sensory and intellectual.'[2] If we look at the linguistic meaning we will see the phrase '*khabuthat nafsuhu*' which implies 'his soul became heavy' or 'his stomach became ill (to the verge of vomiting)'. These images are appropriate to the description of filthy suckling leading to both 'a heavy ego' and causing the child to be 'sick from the stomach upwards'.

'Firstly and lastly' means it becomes part of his nature and as a result his limbs act disobediently whether he wishes to or not.

Reflection

The ideas expressed in this section are common to most traditional cultures. Rousseau said:

> The nurse must be healthy alike in disposition and in body. The violence of the passions as well as the humours spoil her milk... The milk may be good and the nurse bad; a good character is as good as constitution. If you choose a vicious person, I do not say her foster child will acquire her vices, but he will suffer for them. Ought she not to bestow on him day by day, along with her milk, a care which calls for zeal, patience, gentleness and cleanliness? If she is intemperate and greedy, her milk will soon be spoilt; if she is careless and hasty what will become of a poor little wretch left to her mercy, and unable to protect himself or complain. The wicked are never good for anything.[3]

The text raises a number of issues. Living in non-Muslim countries, we have to decide about the company our children are allowed to keep during the early years. In my experience, it is not simply that Muslims should keep to themselves and not allow their children to mix. We had a Jewish neighbour who was more careful about what our children ate than many of our Muslim acquaintances. Our son was allowed to go in and out of her house and we never feared corruption through her character or her food. It is true that we were blessed with good neighbours for most of our lives and that not everyone has been that lucky. What is important is that when we make decisions about who comes into our house or where we allow our children to play and eat, we do so remembering that the child is a trust that we are responsible for, and that we are answerable for any corrupting influences.

Discussion

What criteria do you use when you decide where your toddler plays and eats?

'My parents didn't strongly enforce where we played or ate as we were in regular contact with our extended family. When they did choose other places, it would be an environment that had a good ethos built on the values of generosity and kindness where people were welcoming rather than having a feeling that their presence was burdensome. The toddler should be in a place where there are other toddlers so they can interact, play, form relationships and learn to socialise through playing and eating together.'

Zara Nargis, Student, Peterborough

'We shared a living space with my uncle and his kids and so our play mates and friends were mostly our cousins. Later, we expanded our circle a little with a few kids from the neighbourhood. We were never allowed to play on the street, but we were blessed with a big yard that kept us really well entertained. There was huge benefit in not being on the street I think, in one instance at least: Bosnian culture has a very well developed swearing lingo which is used frequently in everyday language—some say that Bosnian is the language that has the most swear words! However, I never actually heard a swear word until I started school at the age of seven and it sounded very alien and ugly to me.'

Bosnian Sister, Sarejevo

'The important thing for me is that the people they go to and eat with have an understanding of the way we eat and that they respect it. It is difficult to make these judgements but I have to just follow the vibes I get from people. Sometimes they are good and sometimes they are not.'

Malin, Parent, Malmo

'We should place our children in environments of play that are beloved to Allāh and His Messenger, away from other children that may perhaps swear or teach them ungodly character traits. The Prophet, upon him be peace, is described by Allāh as being "upon great character." Let us not forget that this character was forged in the deserts and open plains of Banu Sa'ad where as a toddler he, upon him be peace, had much space to play in, plenty of fresh air and was surrounded by people of pure language. Allowing our children time to play in open spaces is far more nurturing than taking them to an indoor play space that offers children nothing other than plastic man-made objects to climb all over; such play spaces offer our children no real understanding or appreciation of the world around them. Giving our children a love of nature from a young age allows them to grow up as those who contemplate and have a direct relationship to that created by Allāh as opposed to that constructed by mankind.'

Umm Abdullah of the Greensville Trust, Liverpool

What should Muslims do about adoption and fostering? Should we take responsibility for caring for children (from Muslim and non-Muslim backgrounds) who are currently looked after by the State?

'We, as a community, must take responsibility for children who are "in care" primarily because one must wish for others what one wishes for oneself and I would have wished for my child to be taken care of by a Muslim family if, may Allāh forbid, he was taken into care.'

Farhat Khan, Business Consultant, Oslo

'The Muslim community has a responsibility to foster and adopt Muslim children so as to instill a Muslim identity during the early years. There is a great shortage of foster carers in certain boroughs in the UK.'

Arslaan Khan, IT Consultant, Wolverhampton

'There has been a steady increase in Muslim children needing adoption. In 2005, in my authority, there were five children of Muslim background adopted. In 2011/12 there were fourteen. The reason for the growth of children in care with a Muslim background is varied. The Muslim population in England has risen to about 2.4 million and between 2004 and 2010, the Muslim population grew ten times faster than the rest of the population. It is not surprising that the number of Muslim children in England needing an adoptive home has grown. The statistics from the Office for National Statistics clearly shows that there are not enough adopters from Muslim backgrounds to match the number of Muslim children requiring adoption. It is important to maximize on Muslim families seeking to adopt because Muslim families can impart better coping strategies to cope with racism, challenge media stereotypes and provide positive role models.'

Pamela, Adoption Social Worker, UK

What is it like to adopt a child?

'We faced a number of challenges during the adoption approval process, such as the fear of being rejected or being told that we were not a suitable family, and the reorganizing of our lives around the new potential child. These challenges are generally experienced by any adoptive family. Being a Muslim adoptive parent meant there was a myriad of *fiqh* issues to navigate. At times, they left us wondering whether adoption was entirely compatible with being a Muslim (a crazy thought, but one shared by a couple of the social workers who we met through the process). I remember discussing this with my brother who gave me some really amazing advice. He said, "the worst thing for this child would be to remain in foster care [particularly as a vulnerable Muslim child in a non-Muslim household]. Bringing a child into a Muslim home can only be good." This helped me and my wife to progress through the process with the right intention and as a result we have the honour, pleasure and delight of a new addition to our family, alhamdulillah.'

Abdullah Khan, Site Manager, Milton Keynes

'We embarked on this process wanting to "make a difference" to a child's life but in actual fact a difference has been made to our lives. We are the ones that have been blessed by Allāh with a beautiful adopted son who has enriched our lives and helped us appreciate what we have. Adopting a child was something that I had always wanted to do but I never imagined how it would feel or impact our lives. I am amazed at how natural it all feels and how easy it was to mother a child that I had not given birth to. It was also rewarding to see the impact of the whole adoption process on our birth son who has formed a normal, healthy relationship with his adopted brother. We truly do feel blessed.'

Taeeba Khan, Science Teacher, Milton Keynes

Endnotes

1 Al-Ghazālī, *On Disciplining the Soul*, 79.

2 Bā Saudān, *Simt al-'Uqyān*, 83.

3 Rousseau, *Emile*, 28.

4

EARLY YEARS: EATING

وَبَعْدَ مَا يَعْظُمْ تَجِدْهُ يَشْتَهِي - أَكْلَ الطَّعَامِ دَائِماً لاَ يَنْتَهِي

يُعَلِّمُوهُ الأَكْلَ بِالْيَمِينِ - وَالْبَسْمَلَهْ حَتْماً بِكُلِّ حِينِ

وَلاَ يُبَادِرْ قَبْلَ أَكْلِ صَاحِبِهْ - وَيَأْكُلُ الْعَيْشَ الَّذِي بِجَانِبِهْ

وَيَمْضَغُ اللُّقْمَةَ مَضْغاً مُحْكَمَا - وَلاَ يُسَارِعْ أَوْ يُوَالِي اللُّقَمَا

And after he has grown, you will find him desiring
To eat incessantly and unceasingly
One should teach him to eat with his right hand
And say the basmala[1] dutifully every time

And he should not eat before his companion
And he should eat the food nearest to him
And he should chew his food completely
And not hurry or hasten for the next piece

Commentary

One should teach him to eat with his right hand and say 'in the name of Allāh' dutifully every time. And he should not eat before his companion.

And he should eat the food nearest to him and he should chew on his food completely. And not hurry or hasten for the next piece.

Eating is a physical, spiritual and social act. It has many *ādāb*, etiquettes, pertaining to it. Imām al-Ghazālī, whose thinking is reflected in this text, has a book entitled *Kitāb Ādāb al-Akl*, Manners Relating to Eating. It contains a straightforward discussion of the Prophetic etiquettes of eating and then a section on manners related to eating in company. The spiritual aspects of eating are dealt with in the book, *Kasr al-Shahwatayn*, Breaking the Two Desires.[2] In it, al-Ghazālī explains that: 'The greatest of the mortal vices which a man may harbour is the desire of the stomach.'[3]

The Prophet, upon him be peace, warned against gluttony when he said: 'Do not kill your hearts with excessive eating and drinking, for the heart is like a plant that dies if watered too much.'[4]

The most important *ādāb* of eating have been highlighted in lines 19 to 21 of the poem. The food must be *ḥalāl*. This means it is not from things that have been forbidden such as swine and alcohol and it has been obtained through legitimate means. Beyond being *ḥalāl*, it should be wholesome. We are told in the Quran: 'Eat of the good of the things.'[5] The Imām stated that one should use the right hand, start with the words '*bismillahi raḥmāni raḥīm*,' respect guests and chew our food properly.

It is recommended that we wash our hands before and after eating. There are some weak narrations suggesting that washing before eating banishes poverty and washing afterwards washes away sins. And Allāh knows best. The Messenger, upon him be peace, used to have his food placed on a *sufra* on the ground. A *sufra* was a leather cloth taken on journeys for the travellers to eat from. Eating from a table cloth placed on the ground is more conducive to humility and reminds the eater that he or she is a traveller in this world. The Prophet, upon him be peace, said: 'I do not eat reclining for I am but a slave; I eat as a slave eats and sit as a slave sits.'[6] One of the etiquettes of eating is 'to have the intention when eating of strengthening oneself in obedience to God, so as to be obedient through food and not to seek gratification and luxurious living through food.'[7] One should eat from that which is closest, except in the case of fruit where one can eat from any part of the plate. One must not blow on food. If it is hot, you should wait patiently until it cools. When eating dates, you should eat an odd number and keep the date stones separate once you have eaten the fruit. One should keep each mouthful of food small and chew it completely before taking another.

One should always be content with the food and not complain about it. However, if you find something distasteful, it should be put to the side without comment. These etiquettes and the etiquettes of drinking, preparing and serving food are all found in al-Ghazālī's *Manners Related to Eating*.

Reflection

There are three important things that come to mind when I reflect on these lines and my own upbringing. My parents were very English. We were expected to listen carefully to the Queen's speech on Christmas Day, heat the teapot before putting in tea leaves, use a knife and fork correctly and to never leave the table without permission. Some of these very English etiquettes continue to be important and others have been long forgotten and abandoned (standing for the Queen's speech was one of the first to go). The first two issues relate to the adoption or abandonment of customs and norms that are not directly from the Islamic tradition. All cultures have unwritten rules about eating, particularly in company. Politeness at meals is a constant reminder of the need for politeness in all other forms of interaction. Often there is a hierarchy implied in the seating. The values of a society are strongly expressed through eating. This is why, in Islam, it is normal for several people to eat from the same plate implying brotherhood, love and equality. In some cultures, burping, within reason, at a meal is considered a sign of enjoyment of the meal and a compliment to the cook. In other cultures it is considered rude. My question is 'how do we, as a multicultural community, develop table manners that are consistent with Islamic principles but respect each other's cultural tradition?'

The second issue is directly connected to the first. The concept of *'urf*, social custom, has a special role in the Islamic code of ethics and is at the heart of the question above. *'Urf* is a term used for a custom that people practice voluntarily from an unbroken tradition going back many years or centuries, and which does not contradict the principles of Islamic belief and practice. The Messenger was commanded:

خُذِ الْعَفْوَ وَأْمُرْ بِالْعُرْفِ وَأَعْرِضْ عَنِ الْجَاهِلِينَ

Hold to forgiveness; command what is right ('urf); But turn away from the ignorant. (Al-Aʿrāf 7:199)

Al-Qurṭubī says the words *'urf* and *ma'rūf* both mean a 'good habit with which the intellect is content and the soul is satisfied.' Where customs, etiquettes and norms do not contradict the Islamic sources, they should be respected. This is very important in the context of bringing up children in the West.

The third issue is the connection between nourishment and learning. The introduction of breakfast clubs in the educational authority in which I work saw an increase in school attendance, and anecdotal evidence suggests an improvement in behaviour and attainment of many of the most vulnerable children in those particular schools. This was reflected in America when a similar programme was introduced. The Food Research and Action Center reported: 'Studies conclude that students who eat school breakfast increase their math and reading scores as well as improve their speed and memory in cognitive tests.'[8] With recent austerity cuts, this project has been scrapped. I am convinced this is a false economy and we will see the negative consequences of this decision in years to come.

Discussion

How important are mealtimes to the process of a child's social and physical development?

"For me, mealtime was like a communion, a time to share something with my family (though I was often told off for only eating bread and being too picky). I learned from my grandfather that mealtimes are a time for being thankful and appreciating what was on the table and remembering that our Creator sustains us. When he visited from Chile, he surprised us all by saying grace before every meal."

Ricardo Lemus, Disability Activist, Copenhagen

"I think meal times with the family are very important for the child's development. Sharing food brings about a sense of love. Coming together over food, I believe, always leaves good memories in a child. Especially if you share sweet food like 'cakes', 'flans' and all other sweet things as this brings more love and unity amongst the family."

Aminah Hussain, Teacher, Oxford

"The first piece of furniture we bought for our house was the dining table. Mealtimes are the most important time for the family. They teach our children how to sit and eat properly. They provide a chance to catch up with their parents and others and teach them how to make conversation. They provide opportunities for children to 'open up' if they need to talk to us. Eating together encourages the children to eat more healthily and to finish their food."

Saneeya Khan, IT Project Manager, Birmingham

What Western customs should we encourage our children to adopt?

"We should adopt the passion for equality, tolerance for other cultures, table manners, the importance of queuing, saying 'good morning', parking considerately and being environmentally friendly. These are all things that are customary in the West."

Group of Students from Birmingham, Parenting Workshop

"Many of the 'Western' customs, virtues and norms are absolutely in line with Islamic belief and practice: for example, the enjoining of good and the forbidding of evil or the importance of family and friendship. It is important to highlight the commonality we have with the wider community so that our children feel less 'foreign' and interact well with people."

Sasha and Abdul Azeem Clime, New to Islam, Glasgow

"Instead of being scared of new customs and practices, we should realise what good they contain and avoid what bad they have. This is true of non-Muslim customs that we have not encountered before. The interaction with the child is the most important thing, not just allowing or forbidding a child a particular thing."

Ricardo Lemus, Disability Activist, Copenhagen

Endnotes

1 That is to say, '*bismillāhi raḥmāni raḥīm*' 'in the name of God, Most Gracious, Most Merciful.'

2 Al-Ghazālī, *On Disciplining the Soul*, 106.

3 Ibid, 106.

4 Ibid, 109.

5 Al-Naml, 23:51.

6 Related by Aḥmed ibn Ḥanbal in the *Book of Zuhd*.

7 Abū Ḥāmid Muḥammad ibn Muḥammad Al-Ghazālī, *On The Manners Relating to Eating*, trans. D. Johnson-Davies (Cambridge: The Islamic Texts Society, 2000), 5.
8 "School Breakfast Program", Food Research and Action Center, accessed March 19, 2013, http://frac.org/wp-content/uploads/2009/09 school_breakfast_program_fact_sheet.pdf.

5

EARLY YEARS: LIVING SIMPLY

وَيَأْكُلُ الْيَابِسَ مِنَ الطَّعَامِ - تَعَلُّماً بَحْتاً بِلاَ إِدَامِ
حِيناً فَحِيناً فِي الْعَشَاءِ وَالْغَدَا - كَيْلاَ يَرَى الإِدَامَ حَتْماً أَبَدَا
وَأَنْ يُجَنِّبَهُ فُنُونَ الزِّينَهْ - وَجُمْلَةَ الْمَلاَبِسِ الرَّزِينَهْ
وَيَكْسُهُ لَوْنَ بَيَاضِ الْقُطْنِ - حَتَى بِهِ عَنْ غَيْرِهِ يَسْتَغْنِي
وَإِنْ طَلَبْ مَنْقُوشاً أَوْ مُلَوَّنَا - يَقُولُ ذَاكَ لِلنِّسَاءِ لاَ لَنَا
لِبَاسُ أَهْلِ الْفِسْقِ وَالتَّخْنِيثِ - وَأَحْمَقٍ وَفَاجِرٍ خَبِيثِ
وَلاَ يُنَعَّمْ جِسْمُهُ بِمَلْبَسِ - طُولَ الْمَدَى وَلاَ فِرَاشٍ أَمْلَسِ
بَلْ كُلُّ مَا كَانَتْ بِهِ خُشُونَهْ - فَإِنَّهُ أَخَفُّ لِلْمُؤُونَهْ
يُصَلِّبُ الأَعْضَا وَلاَ يُبَالِي - بِالْمَشْيِ أَوْ بِسَائِرِ الأَعْمَالِ
وَيُمْنَعُ النَّوْمَ النَّهَارَ قَطْعَا - خَوْفَ الْكَسَلْ أَوْ يَتَّخِذْهُ طَبْعَا

And he should eat of food that is dry
So he becomes accustomed to it in its purest form
Occasionally for lunch or for supper
So that he does not think it must always be luxurious

And keep him away from various forms of adornment
And all types of expensive clothes
And clothe him in white cotton
So that he feels he is not in need of any other

And if he asks for embellished or coloured (clothes)
Say that is for women and not for us
Clothes of the sinful, the effeminate,
Foolish, debauchee, evil

He should not pamper his body with
Soft clothes and silken bedding
And everything that has coarseness
Will be lighter as provision

It strengthens the limbs
And makes his limbs resilient
So he is bothered not by walking or any other actions
He should always be prevented from sleeping in the day,
Fearing laziness or that it becomes a habit

Commentary

And he should eat of food that is dry so he becomes accustomed to food in its purest form.

Bā Saudān tells us we should not allow our children to grow accustomed to luxury. He suggests that if they do get used to comfort, they will always strive to attain it and in doing so, they will waste their time and develop questionable behaviour, possibly falling into the *ḥarām*, illicit. According to Imām al-Ramlī, the child should become accustomed to food that is 'dry' and 'pure', using the words *baht* which means pure and 'without *idām*' which means 'without condiment.' He tells us we should give the child bread 'without *idām*.' *Idām* is defined as 'that which is eaten with bread' as in the *ḥadīth*, 'vinegar is a blessed condiment' and 'the master of the condiments of this world and the next is meat.'[1] 'Becoming accustomed to food without *idām*' means becoming accustomed to eating bread on its own. It reflects the *ḥadīth* 'honour bread.' Al-Munāwi explains that you should 'honour it above all other types of food because honouring it is the expression of satisfaction at [Allāh's] provision and lack of desire to seek luxury or increase.'[2] Al-Ghazālī says: 'He should be made to enjoy giving the best food to others and encouraged to pay little heed to what he eats and to be content with its coarser varieties.'[3]

And keep him away from various forms of adornment.

Zīna is translated as 'adornment'. Al-Munāwi defines it as 'beautification of something by means of something else and may include clothing, ornaments or posture. It is also said that it is 'delight of the eye where it cannot see the interior of the thing that has been adorned.'[4] We are told to keep our children away from *zīna*.

Razīna means 'expensive' and includes silk. The child should be made to wear plain white clothes. This is based on the *ḥadīth*: 'Wear white clothes and shroud your dead in them for surely they are the most beloved clothes to Allāh.'[5] It is said that they are the most beloved to Allāh because they are simple, do not attract tribulations through jealousy and keep the wearer away from ostentation. These are all characteristics children should be encouraged to adopt as part of their *tarbiyya*, education.

And if he asks for embellished or coloured (clothes), say that is for women and not for us.

Manqūsh, literally means 'engraved' or 'sculptured' but here it is translated as embellished. By telling the child 'that is for women', one indicates that certain types of garments and adornment are permitted for women but not for men. These include silk and gold. The phrase 'that is for women' is to encourage the child to be able to differentiate between the *ḥalāl*, permitted and the *ḥarām*, forbidden.

(Keep him away from the) clothes of the sinful, the effeminate, foolish, debauchee, evil.

'Effeminate' here refers to men who imitate women, an act which is forbidden according to the *ḥadīth*: 'Allāh curses men who imitate women and women who imitate men.'[6]

And everything that has coarseness will be lighter as provision.

This life is just a journey. The less we carry with us, the easier it is to travel. Another meaning of the verse is 'less burdensome' and may refer back to simple white cotton clothes. Simple clothes are less of a physical burden as they require less preparation and maintenance, and are less of a spiritual burden as they are less likely to induce qualities such as ostentation and vying for the temporal world. And Allāh knows best.

It strengthens his limbs and makes his limbs resilient.

This verse implies that we should encourage his or her physical growth through exercise so that he or she is able to carry out the required worldly and religious duties, 'so he is bothered not by walking or any other actions.'

Reflection

Bread in colloquial Arabic is called *'aysh*, which means 'life'. *'Aysh* is used in some parts of Iraq to refer to rice. I remember being invited to the house of a brother from Pakistan with the phrase 'please come around for *roti* (bread).' All of these statements imply that there is a simple basic staple food around which our life should rotate. It has spiritual significance in that it is the minimum sustenance by which our lives are sustained. The Prophet, upon him be peace, advised that bread should not be cut but broken. The word 'companion' is derived from the Latin 'com' meaning 'with' and 'pannis' meaning bread. The 'companion' is one you would break bread with. My Pakistani friend's invitation to *roti* reflects this concept as well as an invitation to share the spiritual connection with the food and its Creator.

The command in these lines is not to limit the child's eating experiences by cruelly starving him or her of condiments, but an indication that we should teach children the spiritual and social significance of simple food. A child should learn the difference between good quality organic food and that which has been adulterated by chemicals and additives. The child should learn not to always strive for new and exotic foodstuffs but to learn contentment with what has been provided, whilst respecting and loving the Provider and Sustainer. These are vital lessons in the development of a child.

The advice regarding clothes is quite difficult to reconcile with the pressures young people face in a modern consumer-driven society.

Marketing and advertising puts a great deal of pressure on families to succumb to ever-changing fashion trends. Commercial endorsements of products are rarely made by people chosen for their moral character. To say that 'these are the clothes of the foolish, debauchee and evil people' contradicts the perception that these are the clothes of the rich, famous and 'successful'.

The power of advertising and the pressure of consumerism have been identified by Juliet Schor in her book *Born to Buy*.[7] Her research suggests that children can recognize logos by 18 months, know brand names by two years old and ask for the latest fashions by the age of 6 or 7. After riots in the UK in 2010, the Department for Education asked UNICEF (UK), the UN children's agency, to look at some of the underlying causes. UNICEF had already identified that Britain, when compared with other developed countries, including substantially poorer ones, was at the bottom of a league table on child well-being. The commissioned report identified that 'children actively coveted certain technology and clothing brands.'[8] The choice of brands is not merely restricted to clothes. 'In addition to its role in children's relationships with their peers, materialism has become enmeshed in children's relationships with family and friends.'[9]

The UNICEF report suggests that the attachment to consumer goods, especially clothes, is related not only to the intense pressure of the media, but also to relationships within the home. Where children are happy and content in their relationships with their parents and enjoy quality interaction, the desire for designer labels and fashionable clothes is less. They are less likely to see clothes as a substitute for real love and sharing of activities and positive interaction.

Reflecting on the way my own children have grown up, I feel the best we can do is to concentrate on building a happy home, try to teach them to be discerning and pray for their protection. This is a massive challenge.

Discussion

In the modern advertising-driven world we live in, are there clothes that we should discourage our children from wearing?

'I am shocked by how men can come to the Sacred Mosque wearing the clothes they sleep in or tee shirts with pictures of pop stars. I asked one of them if he would wear this if invited for an audience with the prince. He said "no."'

Sayyid Abdullah al-Haddad, Makka

'When I went on pilgrimage, I was shocked by how women were expected to wear black and cover their faces while men could wear football shirts, tee shirts with pornographic slogans, swearwords and adverts for alcohol. It smacked of hypocrisy.'

English Pilgrim to Makka

'A woman shall not be clothed in with man's apparel, neither shall a man use woman's apparel: for he that doeth these things is abominable before God.'

Deuteronomy 22:5

'Modern clothes are anything but modest and simple. The idea of "less is more" means children are raised with no sense of *haya'*, modesty, and their *fiṭra*, natural disposition, is fading away quicker than ever before. I think it's very important to encourage children to dress modestly and protect their natural innocence.'

Hanna Mustafa, Copenhagen

How do we encourage our children to follow a healthy diet?

'You have to be a good role model and also try to find other good role models. My son's first cola was when he went to the mosque aged about 2 years. Up until that time he only ate wholesome food.'

Gadija Esau, Teacher, East Dunbartonshire

'In every given situation, one should choose what is the most beloved to Allāh and His Messenger. With regards to the toddler, feed him or her food that is the most beloved to Allāh and his Messenger so that this food goes on to be the food he or she desires throughout his or her life. Pumpkin, barley bread and barley soup, cucumber, dates, grapes, raisins and melon were all eaten by our beloved Messenger, upon him be peace. Those who have not grown up eating pumpkin or barley bread find these foods difficult to get accustomed to and will not have such blessed food as part of their diet.

Allāh also mentions an array of other blessed foods in the Quran such as garlic, lentils, onions, ginger and fish. We should prefer to feed our children such food over a happy meal at McDonald's even if it professes to be ḥalal.'

Umm Abdullah of the Greensville Trust, Liverpool

Endnotes

1 Ibn Athīr, *al-Nihāya fī Gharīb al-Ḥadīth* (Beirut: Dar al-Iḥyah al-Turath al-Arabi, no date).

2 Bā Saudān, *Simt al-'Uqyān*, 88.

3 Al-Ghazālī, *On Disciplining the Soul*, 77.

4 Bā Saudān, *Simt al-'Uqyān*, 88.

5 Related by Aḥmed, *ḥadīth* number 2219, al-Tirmidhī, *ḥadīth* number 999 and others.

6 Related by Aḥmed on the authority of Ibn 'Abbās, *ḥadīth* number 3060.

7 Juliet B. Schor, *Born to Buy* (New York: Scribner, 2004).

8 Agnes Nairn, *Child Well-being in the UK, Spain and Sweden: The Role of Inequality and Materialism* (London: Ipsos-MORI Social Research Institute, 2011).

9 Ibid, 6.

6

THE AGE OF DISCRIMINATION

وَإِنْ بَدَتْ أَمَارَةُ التَّمْيِيزِ - وَكُلِّ فَهْمٍ فَاضِلٍ عَزِيزِ
وَصَارَ يَسْتَحِيِ مِنَ الأُمُورِ - فَذَاكَ أَوَّلُ بُدُوِّ النُّورِ
هَدِيَّةٌ مِنْ رَبِّهِ أَهْدَاهَا - عَرَفَ بِهَا الأَشْيَا بِمُقْتَضَاهَا
فَذَاكَ أَوَّلْ وَقْتِ فَهْمِ الطِّفْلِ - أَشْرَقَ بِهَا عَلَيْهِ نُورُ الْعَقْلِ

When the signs of discernment
And blessed subtle understanding appear
And he becomes shy of matters,
It is the first sign of the Light

Which is a gift gifted by his Lord
He knows, by it, things as they should be
That is the first moment in the child's understanding
That the light of intellect ('aql) ascends upon him

Commentary

When the signs of discernment and blessed subtle understanding appear. And he becomes shy of matters.

Bā Saudān says: 'Discernment, *tamyīz*, is differentiation between similar things. The scholars define the age of discernment as the time when the child is able to differentiate between that which will harm him and that which will benefit him. Some say that discernment is an intellectual ability that we use to extract meanings. It has also been said that it is the visualisation of the meaning from the words of the speaker.'[1]

When the child is able to discern what is harmful and what is beneficial, he or she holds back from disliked actions. *Hayā*, modesty means 'to hold back' or 'be reticent'. When the ability to discern appears, the child becomes reticent about doing actions which are bad. In another version of the poem, Imām al-Ramlī says:

> He becomes shy of some matters
> And this is a sign of goodness

Modesty is of two types:

- Intrinsic, which all humans have and this includes the desire to cover one's nakedness.
- Motivated by faith, which is what prevents a believer from going against what Allāh has forbidden.

It is the first sign of the light.

The 'light' refers to intellect, *'aql*. Imām al-Ghazālī draws the link between the ability to discern and the first 'light of the intellect' being gifted to the child. He says:

> When the signs of discretion appear in him he should again be watched over carefully. The first of these is the rudiments of shame, for when he begins to feel diffident and is ashamed of certain things so that he abandons them, the light of the intellect has dawned in him, whereby he sees that certain things are ugly, and different from others, and begins to be ashamed of some things and not others. This is a gift to him from God (Exalted be He!).[2]

The intellect is called 'light' because it guides one away from the deception of this world to the certainty (*yaqīn*) of the next. The Prophet, upon him be peace, said: 'The temporal world (*al-dunya*) is the abode of the one who has no abode. Wealth is the possession of the one who has no wealth. The one who gathers them has no intellect.'[3] The light begins at this point and then develops with time. The intellect helps the person move forward in the world without becoming attached to it. It is for this reason that the Prophet, upon him be peace, told the famous

Companion, Abu Dharr, 'O Abu Dharr, there is no *'aql* (intellect) like preparation.'[4] This implies planning and preparation in a worldly sense, but when looked at in the light of the first *ḥadīth*, we see that it means preparing and planning for this world but without attachment to it. This is a subtle skill that needs nurturing from the moment that this light appears. This is the essence of *tarbiyya*, which was discussed earlier.

Reflection

This section describes the beginning of intellect. The Prophet, upon him be peace, said: 'Address people according to the level of their intellect,' implying that the intellect develops in stages. This is an important principle in teaching. As children develop, we need to extend their language and understanding by monitoring their development and continually stretching them a little further. The writings of Vygotsky have been important in how I apply these principles. In my mind, the Prophetic advice is consistent with Vygotzsky's 'zone of proximal development.' He described it as 'the distance between the actual developmental level as determined by independent problem solving and the level of potential development as determined through problem solving under adult guidance, or in collaboration with more capable peers.'[5] As the intellect develops, the person responsible for the child's *tarbiyya* should be constantly aware of what the young person is able to do independently and what he or she can do with help. This should be borne in mind in relation to tasks related to behaviour (*adab*), language or cognition and knowledge. The adult should push the young person a little further each time and in doing so, develop the intellect. The following sections describe some of the principles of developing the intellect, including exposure to the Quran from an early age, the etiquette of teaching, the need for play and relaxation and the need for the child to learn the consequences of his or her actions.

Al-Ghazālī and others identify 'modesty' as one of the traits that indicate the onset of intellectual development. Consistent with other traditions, he implies it is a noble trait that should be developed and encouraged. It is one of the key characteristics of all the Abrahamic faiths. The Jewish concept of *Tzniut* can be best explained as modesty in character and behaviour and is connected to the command to 'walk humbly with God.'[6] The concept of *Tzniut* in Rabbinical literature, like *ḥayā*, in the Islamic tradition, is developed into a dress code and a code of behaviour, especially between the genders. Among the biblical commands that seem to have been forgotten in debates about female apparel is: 'For if a woman does not cover her head, she might as well have her hair cut off; but if it is a disgrace for a woman to have her hair cut off or her head shaved, then she should cover her head.'[7] It is sad that the issue of modesty has become politicised. I recently met children who were penalised for not wanting to shower naked. The argument of the school and the political party ruling that particular country was that nudity was part of their tradition and those who do not respect their culture should leave. The country claiming Christian heritage has certainly misunderstood its own roots.

Discussion

How can we protect the chastity of our children and inculcate the values of modesty?

'The nurturing of modesty in our children, like all desired traits, requires that they be first demonstrated in ourselves. As Shakespeare said: "The most eloquent form of speech is action." Modesty is seen to be amongst the actions of the spiritual heart. It originates in the heart's awareness of Allāh and the possible shame that would be incurred in doing that which is displeasing to Him. This realisation is then manifested outwardly in a form of action.

It is this spiritual awareness, and consciousness of heart within ourselves that needs particular attention, for then can our children go on to imbibe modesty for themselves. The modesty we have in our relationship with Allāh will make effective the modesty we seek for our children to have.

For each virtue there is a limit, in that too much of it can bring adverse effects, like too much kindness could mean a loss of discipline. However, the Holy Prophet exempted modesty. Once a man questioned him about what he perceived as excessive modesty from his brother. The Holy Prophet replied, "Leave him! For modesty observed in any regard is blessed."'

Thaqib Mahmood, Lecturer on Classical Islamic Disciplines, Oxford

'Locking away our girls from any potential harm does not work. I have been petrified about exposing my teenage daughter to a society that seems to be becoming more bohemian. However, now that my daughter is coming to the end of her university years, I see that she has adopted more of an Islamic lifestyle. I believe this has been down to our re-enforcement of religious values that has helped nurture her relationship with God and thus allowed her to say 'no' to the extremes of teenage behaviour.'

Anonymous Parent

Endnotes

1 Bā Saudān, *Simt al-'Uqyān*, 95.

2 Al-Ghazālī, *On Disciplining the Soul*, 6.

3 Related by Aḥmed on the authority of 'Āisha, may Allāh be pleased with her, and considered authentic by al-Suyūṭī and others.

4 Related by al-Ṭabarānī on the authority of Abū Dharr and considered to be sound by al-Suyūṭī.

5 L.S Vygotsky, *Mind in Society: Development of Higher Psychological Processes* (Cambridge: Harvard University Press, 1978), 86.

6 Micah 6:8.

7 Corinthians 11:5.

7

DEVELOPING THE INTELLECT: ADHERENCE TO THE QURAN

فَيُلْزِمُوهُ الدَّرْسَ لِلْقُرْآنِ - فَإِنَّهُ عِلْمٌ عَظِيمُ الشَّانِ

He should make him adhere to the study of the Quran
For it is knowledge of mighty status

Commentary

He should make him adhere to the study of the Quran.

Imām al-Ghazālī says: 'Next he should be busy at school learning the Quran, the Traditions, and tales of devout men, so that the love of righteousness may take root in his heart.'[1] We have already discussed the connection between *adab*, character, and the Quran in the context of the *ḥadīth*; 'the Quran is Allāh's banquet (*ma'daba*).' Once the child has developed discernment, he or she is now ready for direct teaching. The first thing to be taught should be the Quran as it is the primary source of Islamic knowledge (*'ilm*) and because learning the *adab* of studying the Quran sets a pattern for more general study. Balfaqīh explains that the Quran should be the first thing the child hears. The mother of my own teacher read the whole Quran from memory while she was feeding him. She would recite the Quran from beginning to end so that by the time he had been weaned, he had heard it many times and was very familiar with it.[2] Balfaqīh continues that the first statement of the Quran should be the phrase '*bismillāhi raḥmāni raḥīm*', 'in the Name of God, Most Gracious, Most Merciful'. This has been discussed previously as one of the *ādāb* of eating. Then the child should be taught the Opening Chapter, known as *al-Fātiḥah* so that 'Allāh opens up his heart.'[3]

The *ādāb* of studying the Quran should become one of the transferrable skills and etiquettes that the child should use for the rest of his or her life in all areas of study. These etiquettes have been compiled by Imām al-Nawawī in his book *Al-Tibyān fi Ādāb Hamlat al-Qurān,* which has been translated into English as *Etiquette with the Quran*.[4]

Among the *ādāb* the student should show are the following:

- He should study from the best teacher available. It has been said that 'this knowledge is religion, so examine well he from whom you take your knowledge.'[5]
- 'The student must look to his teacher with the eye of respect, believe in his competence completely, and his superiority over his contemporaries, since this makes it more likely that one will benefit from him.'[6]
- The student should take care of his appearance.
- He or she should enter and exit the class showing good manners, including greeting and not sitting between people except with their permission.
- The student should not raise his voice, laugh or speak without need and should always be attentive of the teacher.
- He or she should be patient with the teacher even if the teacher is moody. 'Whoever is impatient with the humiliation of learning will spend his life in the blindness of ignorance.'[7]

The emphasis in the poem remains on *adab*. Al-Ramlī says that along with the Quran, the child should stay away from everything that 'leads to a reduction in manners (*adab*).'

Reflection

The way one approaches study is important. The way one sits, dresses and holds a pencil influences learning. One's self esteem and one's respect for the teacher are important internal etiquettes. This section of the poem deals with two very important aspects of the learning environment. The Quran should be the starting point of any Islamic curriculum. It should be both a subject in the curriculum and a reference for other aspects of the syllabus and part of the overall ethos of the school.

The poem clearly links the Quran with *adab*. Here, it implies *adab* with the Quran, Allāh, oneself, one's teacher and as a consequence of inculcating these within oneself, general *adab* with the world around you.

Imām al-Nawawī's description of the *adab* of studying is a vital resource for anyone who wants to understand teaching and learning from an Islamic perspective.

Discussion

How can we instil the Quran in the upbringing of our children?

'The scholars of Ḥadramaut say the strongest tool in child-rearing is their eyes; they act based on what they see. From this principle, as well as from experience, we understand that instilling the Quran in the upbringing of our children will only be achieved if those around them have an attachment to the Quran. They reflect what is around them.'

Zara Nargis, Student, Peterborough

'Show them our love and passion for the Quran.
Tell them why we love the Quran so much.
Tell them stories from the Quran.
Speak about the people who memorised the Quran.
Mention the biographies of the great reciters.'

Muhammad Aslam, City of Knowledge Academy, Birmingham

'When I was growing up, I did not understand the Quran at all. I just knew it was a sacred book and that I had to learn to read it. I wish I had been told what it really was. Children should be told of the sanctity of the book and the message in it and most importantly about our relationship with the Quran. They should be told at a young age what the Quran is so that they may have awe and love for it. In Tarim, the first lesson of the day is the study of the Quran. From this, children see its importance. The peer pressure to succeed is related to the Quran and excelling in its study.'

Huma Abbasi, Religious Studies Teacher, Oxford

Endnotes

1 Al-Ghazālī, *On Disciplining the Soul*, 77.

2 This is a reference to al-Ḥabīb Aḥmed Mashūr al-Ḥaddād, who was one of the greatest scholars

of the last generation.

3 Ḥussain bin ʿAbdul Qādir Balfaqīh, *Taʿlīq wa Bayān fī Sharḥ Riyāḍatul Ṣibyān* (Beirut: Dār al-Hāwi, 2002), 66.

4 Abu Zakaria Mohiuddin Yahya bin Sharaf al-Nawawī, *Etiquette with the Quran*, trans. Musa Furber (Berkeley: Starlatch Press, 2003).

5 Ibid, 21.

6 Ibid.

7 Ibid.

8

DEVELOPING THE INTELLECT: KEEPING THE MIND BUSY

أَيْضاً وَشُغْلُ شَاغِلُ قَلْبَ الصَّبِي - عَنْ كُلِّ مَا يُوجِبُ نَقّصَ الأَدَبِ

Also busy the heart of the child from
that which leads to reduction in manners

Commentary

Also busy the heart of the child from that which leads to reduction in manners.

The word heart (*qalb*) and intellect (*'aql*) are interchangeable in some contexts. This line suggests we should stretch the mind and not allow it to become occupied with things that are of no benefit. The teacher should not allow the child to become engrossed with things that lead to poor manners or disrespectful behaviour.

Reflection

This section of the poem is about allowing the child's mind to grow. It specifically warns against 'that which leads to reduction in manners.' I am often asked whether we should allow our children to watch television or play video games. The answer is in these lines and those that follow. All things that lead the child to poor behaviour or bad manners should be avoided. Many children after playing video games re-enact the game.

Those who watch poor role models on television often repeat the kind of language they hear. What they see or hear on the television becomes the norm. I am not a mufti who can issue edicts on the permissibility of television and other modern media but I know that these guidelines will certainly help in deciding which programmes and games are acceptable. Programmes that encourage poor manners should not be watched.

The other interesting point in this section is the reference to 'keeping the mind busy.' The idea of a 'busy mind' or a 'busy brain' is not a medical term but is widely used by pseudo-medical bloggers, lifestyle gurus and those interested in Buddhism and meditation. One web definition describes the busy brain as 'a mental state that includes racing thoughts, anxiety, lack of focus, and sleeplessness.'[1] Classical scholars, like al-Ghazālī, warn us against allowing harmful images, sounds and smells to enter our bodies through the sensory portals. He says they pollute the heart and are extremely difficult to remove. 'Lack of focus' and 'racing thoughts' are damaging to the developing intellect and can be avoided by avoiding things which 'busy the mind' in a pointless and directionless manner. The idea that we can 'train' the mind (that is, give it *adab*) is not unique to this Ghazalian approach. When I worked as a teacher of children with dyspraxia and related disorders, I found the Brain Gym approach was very beneficial. According to the Brain Gym International website, Brain Gym is based on the principle that 'moving with intention leads to optimal learning.'[2] Carrying out certain movements prior to learning leads to better co-ordination, especially eye-hand co-ordination, stimulates learning and storing and retrieval of information. It was developed from the work of Paul Dennison, a specialist reading teacher in East Los Angeles, during the 1960s and 70s. He researched ways of helping children with learning difficulties and developed a series of drills and exercises which are thought to train the mind in the same way a gym workout trains the body. Although most of the research does not meet the standards expected in neuroscience, I have seen benefits when I have used such exercises with my pupils.

The lines that follow this section talk about the need for relaxation between learning sessions. They suggest the child needs to have regular breaks from study and opportunities to relax and have fun. The means of relaxation should be *ḥalāl*. In particular, physical activity is recommended, as it brings about other developmental benefits. Regular exercise is recommended in Islam. The Prophet, upon him be peace, said: 'The believer who is physically strong is better and more beloved to Allāh than the believer who is physically weak.'[3] He, upon him be peace, also said: 'The body has rights upon you.'[4] One of these rights is that you exercise it and do not allow it to become weak and unfit.

Discussion

What ways can we develop the mind of a child?

'The most practical technique is to learn a musical instrument as this requires mastery of motion while using their senses to refine their ability. The next best exercise is to learn a language.'

Jamil Aslam, IT Consultant, Glasgow

'Play chess and other board games that require careful thought and develop their intellect.'

Anonymous

'Expose children to structured arguments with language that extends their vocabulary. Questions like "What do you think?" and "Why did that happen?" are important.

Gadija Esau, Teacher, East Dunbartonshire

'They should be encouraged to be creative, spontaneous and use their imagination. They need to read quality literature.'

Zahid Hanif, Parent, Glasgow

'In bringing up children, can watching television, playing video games and other technology be considered a cultural norm (*'urf*)?

It is the norm for everyone to have a TV and computer games. We have either of these. We do not have a TV and everyone finds us "strange". People wonder how we survive without a TV. I think it is a norm but not *'urf* and it is certainly not something essential.'

Javeria Khatoon

'The value of having a television, computer games and tablet computers is based on how we use them. Allowing a child to be a part of this growing technological world helps the child feel part of modern society. It is something we should not be afraid of and may be considered *'urf*.'

Aminah Hussain, Teacher, Oxford

"*'Urf* has to be something beneficial and culturally enriching. If something is harmful, how can it be considered an *'urf*? Discussing the value of television is like discussing whether smoking is permissible or impermissible. As medicine progresses, we can see the damage that smoking does to the body. The American Paediatric Association said children under the age of two should not watch TV because it hampers their linguistic development by depriving them of human interaction and damaging their concentration. TV is certainly more harmful than beneficial. In my view, it might be permissible for older children, but, based on medical evidence, it would be hard to say it is *ḥalāl* for young children."

Dr. Daniel Jackson, Child Psychiatrist, Yardley

Endnotes

1 "Busy Brain," accessed July 15, 2010, http://www.wordspy.com/words/busybrain.asp.

2 "Mission statement," accessed July 15, 2010, http://www.braingym.org

3 Related by Muslim, *ḥadīth* number 2052.

4 Related by Aḥmed on the authority of 'Abdullāh bin 'Amr.

9

DEVELOPING THE INTELLECT: LEARNING CONSEQUENCES

وَإِنْ ضَرَبْ مُعَلِّمُ الصِّبيَانِ - أَوْ وَالِدٌ بَعْضاً مِنَ الْوِلْدَانِ

فَلاَ يَكُنْ مِثْلَ النِّسَاءِ يبْكِي - وَيَشْتَفِعْ بِغَيْرِهِ وَيَشْكِي

فَعَادَةُ الشُّجْعَانِ أَنْ لاَ يَذْكُرُوا - كُلَّ الَّذِي جَرَى لَهُمْ بَلْ يَصْبِرُوا

And if the boy's teacher strikes him
Or the father or either of his parents,
He should not cry like women
Or seek intercession through another or complain

Commentary

And if the boy's teacher strikes him ... he should not cry like women do.

Balfaqīh says that 'hitting [a child] is neither completely forbidden nor required, except in extreme need.' He explains that in these extreme circumstances, a boy must be told 'not to cry excessively or to try and manipulate' the parent or teacher's emotions by exploiting the fact that no normal person actually enjoys hitting a child, especially not their loved ones. He suggests that crying 'is the weapon of women to affect emotions. It has no place in manhood; men do not cry except out of fear of Allāh or gentleness towards the weak or sadness over death.'[1]

Reflection

I fear that this is the area where my upbringing and training as a teacher may bring me into conflict with Muslim cultural norms more than any other topic in this book. I remember my shock and horror when an Egyptian lady came up to me with her son who was about to join my class saying, 'He is like your child, hit him if you need to.' I never hit my children. I was never hit by my parents or my shaykhs. In fact, the only corporal punishment I received was at my English Grammar School. My experience of *tarbiyya* from my parents and shaykhs was built on love and mercy. These early personal experiences undoubtedly shaped my interpretation of these principles.

I later learned that the experience of most Muslims attending traditional *madrasas*, mosques and supplementary schools may have been very different to mine. Many early migrant communities tried to replicate the education of their homelands. As a consequence, many young British Muslim children saw the mosque as a backward, dirty place where sitting on the floor was the norm and being hit was standard punishment for not meeting the expectations of the teacher. This would be in direct contrast to the warm, friendly and stimulating environment of their secular state schools. As Muslim communities became stronger in Britain, these two worlds came closer as the community began to establish their own schools that would adopt secular approaches, including a new perspective on child protection. Debate about the use of corporal punishment intensified and I, as a newly qualified Muslim teacher, had to consider the best way of disciplining children. My natural inclination was against hitting children. I found no precedent in the practice of the Prophet, upon him be peace. He never struck women or children. Although I accepted it was permissible under certain circumstances, I knew these drastic steps were because other methods had failed or probably not been applied properly. When we are told to encourage children to pray at seven and hit them at ten if they neglect the prayer, it is clear that during the intervening years and well before the command even becomes relevant, there should be other means of encouraging the child to pray. I witnessed my own children 'playing' prayer as soon as they could walk. Congregational prayer was part of family life and so there was no need to 'force them' to pray and as a consequence no need to hit them for neglecting the prayer. I understand the statement 'hit them' to emphasise the importance of prayer in a child's development and not a 'command', or even permission to abuse or hurt children. I accept that my interpretation is one of a non-scholar. It is personal and made under the influence of my own Western upbringing within a wider debate about values.

To understand this debate fully, we need to look at it in an historical context. During the 1940s and 50s, research into discipline was descriptive, focusing on examining contemporary parenting patterns. It later moved from describing child rearing practices to examining the effectiveness of hitting, and then into the realm of the psychological effects of corporal punishment. The debate was inconclusive. Some indicated corporal punishment was both effective and desirable,[2] and other studies suggested it was ineffective and in many cases damaging.[3] The current phase of this debate is now the politicisation of the issue and re-examination of the values underlying our culture and society. A growing number of countries, including Denmark, Israel and Germany have passed laws prohibiting parents from hitting their children. When delivering training on this book in Denmark, the politicization of the issue was clear. If I were to quote any Islamic source permitting or appearing to encourage hitting children, I would be in conflict with the law of the land and would 'prove Islam is an alien culture that is incompatible with the West.' The discussion is no longer about effective parenting, but about where we stand in the 'clash of cultures'.

The positive side of the politicisation of the debate is that it brings the discussion back to values and principles. It makes us question the very nature of education and the foundation of our society. Therefore, I do not feel apologetic about my interpretation. The foundation of discipline, and the value on which our education is based, in my view, is the Prophetic statement that: 'He who does not respect our elders or show mercy to our young is not one of us.'[4]

Discussion

What role does hitting children play in discipline and child development?

'You have to consider that we are training our children. They know nothing of the world or how to behave. If you start a new job and do something wrong because you haven't grasped everything, you wouldn't expect a smack off your boss, would you? Then why hit children who are learning? You explain to them what they have done wrong and explain the correct way to do it ... without smacks (violence). Praise them when they do right and don't reward bad behaviour. Emphasise the good behaviour, not the bad.'

'Tricky' on Ummah Forum

'He that spareth his rod hateth the son: but he that loveth his chasteneth him betimes.'

Proverbs 13:24

'I believe that parenting is about communication. If a parent resorts to hitting their child, this is a failure on the parent's side. Why should it come down to hitting? A parent should have a tool box of punishments and use each one according to the situation. If you decide to give your child a smack on the bottom then it should be a means of punishment and not as a frustrated attack on your child.'

Dr Mughees Khan, Birmingham

'Smacking is certainly a necessary measure in your parenting tool box. They need to know there are lines they cannot cross.'

Abdullah Khan, Site Manager, Milton Keynes

'I believe "behaviour is a language". I know for sure that behaviour is a form of expression when there are areas of concern in another part of a child's life. Firstly, talking to the child is very important, asking leading questions like: "What made you react like that? It's unlike you." This helps us to understand it rather than jump to punish it. Secondly, ensuring "positive choice of language" is used. The aim is for children to make a choice and depending on the wording of what the adult asks, the child will respond positively and follow the instruction without quarrel or confrontation. Thirdly, "reward positive behaviour continually and consistently." This takes emphasis away from negative behaviour and places significance on achievement and good manners.'

Smera Hussain, English Teacher, Wolverhampton

Endnotes

1 Balfaqīh, *Taʿlīq wa Bayān*, 71.

2 Diana Baumarind, "A Blanket Injunction Against Disciplinary use of Spanking is not Warranted by the Data," *Paediatrics* 98 (1998): 261–267. Diana Baumarind, "The Discipline Controversy Revisited," *Family Relations* 45 (1996): 405–415.

3 Barbara J. Howard, "Guidance for Effective Discipline," *Paediatrics* 101 (1998), 723–728.

4 Related by al-Tirmidhī, *ḥadīth* number 1019, and Abū Dawūd, *ḥadīth* number 4935.

10

DEVELOPING THE INTELLECT: THE NEED FOR RELAXATION

وَرَاحَةُ الصِّبْيَانِ بَعْدَ الْمَكْتَبِ - أَنْ يَأْذَنَ الْوَلِي لَهُمْ بِاللَّعِبِ

فَإِنَّهُ عِنْدَ الصَّبِي مَحْبُوبُ - وَقَلْبُهُ أَيْضاً بِهِ يَطِيبُ

وَكَثْرَةُ التَّعْلِيمِ مَوْتُ الْقَلْبِ - وَيُذْهِبُ الذَّكَا وَبَعْضَ اللُّبِّ

فَيَطْلُبُونَ لِلْخَلَاصِ حِيلَهْ - تُنْجِي مِنَ التَّعْلِيمِ أَوْ وَسِيلَهْ

(There should be) relaxation for the children after study
When the guardian allows them to play
For it is beloved to the child
And through it, his heart becomes sweet

Too much teaching kills the heart
Causing sharpness and some of the intellect to be lost
Thus they seek a means of escape
To save them from teaching or find an excuse

Commentary

There should be relaxation for the children after study.

The Prophet, upon him be peace, said: 'Allow your hearts relaxation from time to time.'[1] It is reported that his close friend, Abu Bakr, may Allāh be pleased with him, questioned the practice of a group of Companions reading Quran and then reciting poetry, to which the Prophet, upon him be peace, said: 'A time for this and a time for that,' implying intense worship or study should be balanced by permissible relaxation. This is more likely to lead to consistency, which is one of the goals of education. The Prophet, upon him be peace, said: 'The most beloved of acts to Allāh are those which are consistent even if they are few.'[2]

Planned relaxation and recreation increases yearning for learning and allows the intellect to develop. Imām al-Ghazālī says: 'After school, he should be allowed to play in a fashion which gives him some rest after his hard work in class, although he should not be allowed to grow exhausted. To prevent a child from playing and to fatigue him with constant lessons causes his heart to die and harms his intelligence and makes his life so hateful to him that he will cast around for a means of escape.'[3]

The Prophet, upon him be peace, recommended a physically active life. He is known to have swum, wrestled, raced horses and, on at least two occasions, raced his wife. He particularly encouraged swimming, archery and horse riding. He said: 'The physically strong believer is better than the physically weak one.'[4]

Ibn al-Qayyim mentions many benefits of exercise, emphasising its effect on digestion. He says: 'The minimum benefit therein is exercise that assists in the preservation of health and repelling superfluities. As for the significant benefits for which it was prescribed, as means to attain good things of this world and the next, and repelling their evils, that is another matter altogether.'[5]

Thus they seek a means of escape to save them from teaching or find an excuse.

'Excessive lessons packed together without rest between them leads to a lack of appetite for study and burdens the intellect. This is what the poet describes as the death of the heart.'[6] 'Seeking escape' is what drives some students to feign illness or request to use the bathroom when they don't actually need to.[7]

Reflection

The division of a child's experience into 'serious learning' and 'play and relaxation' is something that I don't fully ascribe to. Learning can be fun. It can have an element of play. My training as a teacher was based largely on the approach of Maria Montessori who encouraged play as a means to development. My inclination to the writing of the American philosopher of education John Dewey was confirmed when I discussed his works with a Mauritanian Islamic scholar with whom I had the good fortune to study Jurisprudence in Spain. In recent years, active learning and co-operative learning have become very popular and I have delivered training in these areas. I firmly believe learning should be enjoyable and is most effective when interactive.

There needs to be a balance between giving knowledge the respect it deserves and delivering it in the most effective way possible. The Quran and most of the fundamental Islamic sciences demand a great level of *adab* and therefore, some of the strategies and techniques of co-operative learning may not be appropriate. Most other areas of the child's learning should be delivered in the way that is best for the child. The educator needs to equip himself or herself with as many styles of delivering knowledge as they possibly can. They must also see the child as an individual who has a learning style that is specific to him or her. In my experience, most children who fail to learn do so because the style of teaching does not match their style of learning. Often, taking the time to look at how the child responds to questions and activities can give insight into what is going on in the child's mind.

Discussion

How can we give our children time for some relaxation and fun that is still ḥalāl and will bring about developmental benefits?

'One parent in my study told me that she had taken her children for picnics in almost all the parks in the city. She believes in taking children outdoors for fresh air to enjoy nature.'

Aminah Mah, Researcher, University of Western Australia, Perth

'The best form of relaxation is one that involves plenty of fresh air and getting back in touch with nature. I love swimming and encourage my children to swim. It exercises every part of the body and their mind.

For me, it is the best form of relaxation and I am glad my children enjoy it too.'

Anonymous

'Every child is different. If a child has a particular skill or interest, sport or art for example, where their Islam is not compromised, this should be encouraged. Social interaction is important. Activities should be social, like Scouts. Camping is enjoyable and helps children understand nature and the environment that develops their belief in God. It promotes a sense of responsibility and teamwork. Mosques should provide these types of activities and develop interfaith links with other organisations. They should set up youth activities and clubs which attract young people through these kinds of activities.'

Sasha and Abdul Azeem Clime, New to Islam, Glasgow

'Traditional arts and crafts (such as sewing, knitting, woodwork and weaving) will be of benefit to the child and parent, especially when done together.'

Zahid Hanif, Parent, Glasgow

Should girls be encouraged to pursue an interest in sports?

'The restrictions on women participating in sport or physical activity are more than that of men. All Islamic observances must be followed, regardless of any school policies or social stigmas. Our obedience to our Creator must be given preference over a creature of Allāh.'[8]

Hikmat al-Beiruty

'Girls should participate in sports, but we should facilitate environments that meet the demands of proper clothing, revealing of body shapes, mixing of sexes and so on. There should be no compromise in this. The goal does not justify the means.'

Umm Amina, Housewife, Copenhagen

'My friend argued that girls shouldn't be doing sports outside of the house as this would involve jumping and moving around in front of the opposite gender, all of which could reveal someone's body shape. Now, this is something that I find terribly restricting and I feel I would be doing my body injustice by not being physically active. I feel I have to occasionally do it outside in the beautiful nature that Allāh has created. If I cover up properly, is there anything wrong with doing sports? I don't see anything wrong with that.'

Anonymous Sister

'I used to be very shy and lacked confidence. I did enjoy one or two sports at school but it wasn't until I went to college and started Muay Thai that I really began to grow in confidence and enjoy sport. It had a massive effect on my personality and I think it helped my studies and general life. Surely, Islam couldn't restrict sport, with all these benefits, to boys only!'

Anonymous Sister

'I am very thankful for my father who encouraged me at a young age to pursue martial arts. Despite the mixed gender class I was able to participate fully without compromising my modesty. By pursuing this sport I was able to represent women in Islam, which I believe had a massive effect on non-Muslims and Muslim men. I also later went on to teach the sport to other Muslim women. So if I was restricted at an early age I would not have been this fortunate to achieve what I have today.'

Anonymous Sister

Endnotes

1 Related by al-Daylami and Abu Nuaym with this wording but with a narration related by Muslim that strengthens the *ḥadīth* with the wording 'O Hanzala, an hour for this and an hour for that.'

2 Related by al-Bukhārī, *ḥadīth* number 5223, and Muslim, *ḥadīth* number 210.

3 Al-Ghazālī, *On Disciplining the Soul*, 80.

4 Related by Muslim, *ḥadīth* number 2052.

5 Ibn Qayyim al-Jawziyya, *Medicine of the Prophet*, trans. Penelope Johnstone (Cambridge: Islamic Texts Society, 1998), 180.

6 Balfaqīh, *Ta'līq wa Bayān*, 84.

7 Ibid.

8 Hikmat al-Beiruty, "Muslim Women in Sport," accessed March 19, 2013, http://www.themodernreligion.com/women/w_sport.htm.

11

DEVELOPING THE INTELLECT: THE NEED FOR GENTLENESS AND GOOD ROLE MODELS

وَالرِّفْقُ فِي كُلِّ الأُمُورِ أَحْسَنُ - قَالُوا بِذَا وَصَرَّحُوا أَوْ بَيَّنُوا

وَبَعْدَ مَا يُشْرِقُ نورُ الْعَقْلِ - عَلَى الصَّبِي يُؤْمَرُ أَنْ يُصَلِّي

وَلْيَلْتَزِمْ فِعْلَ الْكِرَامِ الأَوْلِيَا - الْمُتَّقِينَ الصَّالِحِينَ الأَصْفِيَا

وَيَعْتَمِدْ جُلُوسَهُ بَيْنَهُمْ - حَتَّى يُوَافِقَ طَبْعُهُ طَبْعَهُمْ

وَلْيَنْغَرِسْ بِقَلْبِهِ مَا يَسْتَمِعْ - وَيَنْطَبِعْ فِي قَلْبِهِ مَا يَنْطَبِعْ

And gentleness in all matters is best
That is what (the scholars) say, emphasise and explain
And when the light of intellect appears
Upon the child he should be commanded to pray

And he should adhere to acts of the noble ones, the saints
The righteous, doers of good, the pure ones
And he should definitely sit among them
So that his nature becomes like theirs

And he should firmly plant in his heart that which he hears
And what he follows, he will follow with his heart

Commentary

And gentleness in all matters is best.

This is because *al-rifq*, gentleness, is recommended in all states as stated in many traditions. Amongst them is the *ḥadīth*: 'Whenever there is gentleness in something it shines and whenever there is harshness in something it dulls it.'[1]

The word *rifq* means gentleness, friendliness, kindness, graciousness and courteousness. The Prophet, upon him be peace, said: 'Whoever shows *rifq*, gentleness, to his nation, Allāh will show *rifq* to him.' One might say, using the verbal form, *rafaqta al-'Amal* meaning, 'I did the act skilfully or judiciously or delicately.' From this use of the word *rifq*, we can see the connection with the word *adab*, explained earlier. It implies skilfully working out what is appropriate in each situation and state.[2]

In the case of bringing up children, gentleness is part of the Prophetic guidance. He, upon him be peace, said: 'Whenever someone is placed in responsibility over someone and he shows them gentleness, Allāh will show gentleness to him on the Day of Resurrection.'[3] He also said: 'If Allāh wishes goodness for a household, He places gentleness amongst them.'[4] A narration related by al-Darquṭunī explains this further and links it to a *ḥadīth* mentioned earlier regarding relationships between the generations: 'If Allāh wishes goodness for a household he instils in them understanding of the religion, their young respect their elders and He grants them gentleness in their family life, balance in their spending and allows them to see their faults so that they can turn away from them. If He wishes other than that for them, He leaves them like animals without a shepherd.'[5]

And when the light of intellect appears upon the child he should be commanded to pray.

The 'light of intellect' has been discussed earlier in the text. Imām al-Ramlī described its early signs, the most important of which were shyness and modesty. Here, he talks about a later stage of development, where the child is ready for a more formal curriculum and requires a more structured experience. After emphasising the importance of gentleness and relaxation, he talks about the actual content of the child's learning. At this point the child should be ordered to pray. Most jurists consider this to be at the age of seven years old while others link it to the age of discernment. Al-Ghazālī says: 'As he reaches the age of discretion he should not be excused the ritual ablutions and the Prayer, and should be told to fast for a few days during Ramadan, and should be prevented from wearing gold, silk or embroidered clothes. He should be taught about the limits laid down by the Law, and put in fear of theft and unlawful gain and also of lying, treachery and deceit.'[6]

Bā Saudān says that this period of teaching should begin with an explanation of the meaning of *lā ilāhā ilallāh*, 'there is no god but Allāh' and an introduction to the Prophet Muḥammad, upon him be peace, which should include the rudiments of his biography, his status and role in guiding his nation. He should be encouraged to 'adhere to the acts of the noble ones.' 'Adhere', *lizām*, means to 'adopt' and 'burden his ego' by imitating their actions.[7]

And he should adhere to the acts of the noble ones, the saints.

'Acts of the noble ones are those acts that benefit and are performed without any worldly purpose.'[8] These are the 'acts of the *awliyā*', here translated as 'saints'. *Awliyā* is the plural of *walī*, which can be translated as 'friend'. The root of the word *walī* means 'to draw close' or 'to attain proximity' in terms of place or status. *Wilāyāt* (the situation of being a *walī*) has to have two elements, since closeness has to be relative to something specific. Anyone who is close to someone else can be described as a *walī* of the other. *Walī* here means *walī* of Allāh, someone who is close to Allāh. Ibn Ḥajar defines a *walī* as 'a scholar who is constant in obedience and sincere in his worship.'[9] One reaches this status through, first of all, completing the mandates placed upon him by his Lord and then by carrying out supererogatory acts of worship. The Prophet, upon him be peace, relates from his Lord, that He, the Exalted, said: 'Whoever shows enmity to a close friend of Mine, I declare war on him. My slave does not draw close to Me with anything more beloved to Me than that which I have made obligatory upon him. My slave continues to draw close with optional extra acts until I love him. When I love him, I am his hearing with which he hears, his sight with which he sees, his hand with which he grasps and his foot with which he walks. If he asks Me I will definitely give him and if he seeks refuge with Me, I will definitely give him refuge.'[10]

Aḥmed Mubārak said that the role of the *walī* is to guide towards Allāh, and gather people on the path towards Him and abstinence from other than Him. For this reason, the *walī* should be the role model and the child's guide.[11]

The righteous, doers of good, the pure ones.

The poem describes these saints who act as role models for the child. It mentions three attributes. They have *taqwa*, that is, their actions are an expression of the loving awe and respect for Allāh, they are righteous, and pure.

Taqwa has been translated as 'fear of God', 'awareness of God', 'piety', 'righteousness', 'obedience' and 'devotion'. Imām al-Ḥaddād defines it as 'fulfilling the commandments of Allāh and avoiding His prohibitions both inwardly and outwardly while feeling adoration and reverence for Allāh as well as awe, fear and dread.'[12]

'The second of their attributes is that they are righteous. They are known as righteous because they fulfil their duties towards Allāh the Exalted and deliver the rights of humankind.'[13]

They are called 'the pure ones' because their actions are not polluted by defects, weaknesses or gaps, and because of the purity of their hearts, they do not go against what He has requested of them.

And he should definitely sit among them so that his nature becomes like theirs.

The Quran and *ḥadīth* recommend sitting with the righteous people and imitating them. Allāh commanded the Prophet, upon him be peace, to imitate the Prophets who came before him. He, the Exalted, said:

أُوْلَـٰٓئِكَ ٱلَّذِينَ هَدَى ٱللَّهُ فَبِهُدَاهُمُ ٱقْتَدِهْ

Those were the (Prophets) who received Allāh's guidance: Copy the guidance they received. (al-Anʿām 6:90)

With specific reference to the righteous, the Prophet, upon him be peace, informs us that Allāh describes them as: 'People whom sitting with will never lead to wretchedness.'[14] He, upon him be peace, said: 'A person will be on the religion of his intimate friend so look carefully to whom you become close.'[15]

Reflection

When I began my teacher training, I was asked to go to a particular nursery school because they were in need of a male role model. Ever since, I have wondered about the validity of that statement and what effect it had on my career. Simon Brownhill, a lecturer at Derby University, recently published a research paper questioning whether males in the early years bring any added benefit and challenged the notion that young people are influenced by role models.[16] He concluded that footballers, actors and singers are less likely to act as role models or influence the behaviour of young children than a peer who shows particular qualities such as standing up to bullies or excelling in art or sport. The interesting thing about his work is that he points out that the young person has to be able to relate to the role model and identify with some of his or her characteristics. I have used a 'buddy' system to help settle children into new situations and to provide support for children with additional needs. This has usually produced the desired effect. However, behind the buddy system is a teacher or specialist who has chosen the buddy and directed the relationship by providing situations which lead to growth and development. I remain convinced that role models are important and they should include adults and older children. This is consistent with the *ḥadīth* mentioned above and a story I remember one of my teachers telling us many years ago. He talked about a student in Uganda who returned to his remote village where he tended to his cows for most of the day around the hilltops near his home. After weeks of being out of touch with people, he hardly spoke and had even adopted the head movements of the cattle he was looking after. I am not sure of the authenticity of the story but the point the shaykh was making was clear—we are influenced by those around us!

Discussion

Can we be too gentle with our children?

'You can never be too gentle with kids. Even when punishing or disciplining children, you should still do this in a gentle manner. Of course, this may take years of practice and you have to discipline your own ego first and foremost. This requires a lot of patience. But this was the way of our Prophet, upon him be peace, and this is what we should strive for.'

Anonymous

'I must teach my child the disciplines of life, the necessary courtesies, the little laws. But quietly and kindly. With love.'

Pam Brown, American Poet

'Every situation requires a different approach. For example, if your child insists he or she wants to go out, despite your disapproval, you have to be firm and hope that later in life they will understand. It is important you lay down the boundaries when they are young. The time to be gentle is when they are older. Then you can give them plenty of space to make their own decisions. Being harsh does not mean you do not love your children. Being too gentle and laid back can ruin the child when they are older. All situations require a balance between gentleness and firmness.'

Zunara Arshad, Parent, Bradford

'For each virtue there is a limit; too much of it can bring about adverse effects, like too much kindness could mean a loss of discipline.'

Thaqib Mahmood, Lecturer on Classical Islamic Disciplines, Oxford

Endnotes

1 Bā Saudān, *Simt al-'Uqyān*, 104.

2 Ibn Athīr, *al-Nihāya fī Gharīb al-Ḥadīth* (Beirut: Dar al-Iḥyah, no date).

3 Related by Ibn Abi Dunya on the authority of 'Āisha.

4 Related by Aḥmed, al-Bayhaqī and al-Bukhārī in his *Tārīkh* on the authority of 'Āisha.

5 Related by al-Darquṭunī on the authority of Anas.

6 Al-Ghazālī, *On Disciplining the Soul*, 77.

7 Bā Saudān, *Simt al-'Uqyān*, 104.

8 Ibid, 107.

9 al-Ḥabīb 'Alawi bin Tāhir al-Ḥaddād, *'Uqūd al-Almās bi Manāqib al-Ḥabīb Aḥmed bin Hasan al-Aṭṭās* (Singapore: Karaji Press, 1991), 36.

10 Related by Bukhārī, *ḥadīth* number 6502.

11 al-Ḥaddād, *'Uqūd al-Almās*, 38.

12 'Abdullāh ibn 'Alawi al-Ḥaddād, *Taqwa and Knowledge*, trans. Abdul Aziz Ahmed, (Glasgow: Islamic Texts for the Blind, 2010), xiii.

13 Bā Saudān, *Simt al-'Uqyān*, 108.

14 Related by al-Tirmidhī, *ḥadīth* number 3600.

15 Related by al-Bukhārī, *ḥadīth* number 6168 and Muslim *ḥadīth* number 2640.

16 Simon Brownhill, "The 'Brave' Man in the Early Years (0–8): The Ambiguities of being a Role Model" (Paper presented to the University of Derby, Derby, January 20, 2010).

12

KEEPING GOOD COMPANY

وَيَحْتَفِظْ بِهِ عَنِ الْجُهَّالِ - وَكُلِّ أَهْلِ الْفِسْقِ وَالضَّلَالِ

وَمَنْ عُرِفْ بِالْكِذْبِ وَالْخِيَانَةْ - وَكُلِّ مَنْ لَيْسَتْ لَهُ أَمَانَةْ

فَإِنَّ أَصْلَ أَدَبِ الأَخْيَارِ - حِفْظُ الصَّبِي عَنْ صُحْبَةِ الأَشْرَارِ

إِذِ الطِّبَاعُ تَسْرِقُ الطِّبَاعَا - وَكُلُّ مَنْ صَاحَبْ خَبِيثاً ضَاعَا

وَقَدْ أَتَى نَصٌّ عَنِ الرَّسُولِ - بِأَنَّ طَبْعَ الْمَرْءِ كَالْخَلِيلِ

By it he will be preserved from the ignorant ones
And all the people of iniquity and error
And those known for lies and deception
And those who cannot be trusted

For the foundation of the manners of the elite
Is protecting the child from the company of the evil
For nature steals nature
And whosoever accompanies the rotten one has lost

And surely text has come from the Messenger
That the nature of a person is that of his intimate Companion

Commentary

By it he will be preserved from the ignorant ones, and all the people of iniquity and error and those known for lies and deception and those who cannot be trusted.

By taking care to keep the child in good company, the educator prevents the child from sitting with ignorant people. He should protect him from even looking at them, for looking at someone who does ugly acts normalises the act. This is especially true of long term exposure to such people and acts. The *juhāl*, ignorant ones, are those whose actions are not based on knowledge or who believe things contrary to the reality. By sitting with such people, the child may think these acts are good or the belief is correct. This is true of *ahl al-fisq*, people of iniquity, who are defined as those who turn away from holding to the commands of the Law, and also of the *ahl al-dalāl*, people of error, who are those who have veered from the straight path. It also mentions the people known for lies and deception and those who cannot be trusted.

For the foundation of the manners of the elite is protecting the child from the company of the evil.

Bā Saudān says: 'The Gnostics have agreed that the foundation of *adab* and the key to all goodness and the basis for establishing exalted character is keeping company with the elect and avoidance of the company of the wicked. For the company [of the wicked] is a distressing disease and a brewing poison. This is especially true of the child whose heart is in a clear, pure state. For if he is accustomed to good and sitting with the elect, it will be engraved onto his heart, and the opposite if he gets used to evil.'[1]

Reflection

This section is very straightforward and can be summed up through the experiences of someone quite close to me. He was a young man who had gone a little astray in his life. Although he was from a Muslim background, he had not been brought up in a house of practising Muslims. When he faced a spiritual crisis during his twenties, he decided to cut off from his friends. He later told me that this was the biggest step on the path to resolving his internal conflict and finding a path of peace within himself. After cutting off from his peer group, he was able to choose his friends more carefully. Those of his friends who made an effort to maintain their friendship grew close and became more sincere. The others carried on following the path they had chosen. With time, he met some good people and eventually a wife who completed his transformation. He is now the happy father of two teenage children who are well balanced, focused and successful. His statement that 'his friends were the biggest barrier to moving forward with his life' sums up this section. He was also very fortunate. We should try to avoid our children having to face these crises by providing them with the right company and good opportunities as children.

Discussion

Is it wrong to 'manipulate' friendship groups to ensure your child has good role models?

'Personally, I feel it is the correct way for a parent to act. We, as parents, guide our children to healthy eating, healthy living and approved institutions, so why would guiding our child to good company be any different? It is my duty to be aware of my child's company and steer him as necessary.'

Safina Akhtar, Nurse, Peterborough

'I think we need to realise that children are like sponges and they emulate what they see. We need to guide them to mix with the "right" sort of people who have the same outlook as you. I try and encourage my children to attend activities that I know children who have good *adab* will be attending. This might not necessarily mean activities with just Muslims.'

Shaheen, Parent, Peterborough

'The word "manipulate" rings alarm bells for me. To "manipulate" conjures up images of insincerity, and conniving, self-centred behaviour. I believe the parent that would manipulate friendships needs to think about his or her own relationships with people. However, I do believe a mother should seek good friends that would provide a healthy environment for her children. This is different to manipulation. We all want our children to have sound role models. This should be done with sincerity and honesty.'

Umm Isa, Home-Schooling Mother, Peterborough

'Muslim parents are stricter in the West than they would have been "back home". I came from Pakistan when I was eight. My dad says I can only have Muslim friends but I think it is unfair. Muslim friends are not always that good. It is better to have a non-religious friend that is sincere than to have a nominally Muslim friend who is not a nice person. I don't like the way he judges people. He says he trusts us but I don't think he really does.'

17-year-old Anonymous Girl, Glasgow

Endnotes

1 Bā Saudān, *Simt al-'Uqyān*, 114.

13

THE ETIQUETTE OF SPEECH

وَيَمْنَعُوهُ كَثْرَةَ الْكَلَامِ - لِأَنَّهُ مِنْ عَادَةِ اللِّئَامِ

أَيْضاً وَمِنْ أَنْ يَبْتَدِي خِطَابَا - إِلاَّ أَنْ يَكُونَ قَوْلُهُ جَوَابَا

ثُمَّ الْيَمِينَ يَمْنَعُوهُ عَنْهَا - بَتّاً دَوَاماً دَهْرَهُ يَدَعْهَا

وَجُمْلَةَ الأَشْعَارِ وَالأَغَانِي - يُمْنَعُ مِنْهَا دَائِمَ الزَّمَانِ

وَالْبَصْقُ وَالْمُخَاطُ وَالتَّنَحُّمُ - عِنْدَ الْجَلِيسِ لاَ عَلَيْهِ يُقْدِمُ

وَاللَّعْنُ وَالسَّبُّ وَشَتْمُ النَّاسِ - وَالاخْتِلاَطُ بَيْنَ ذِي الأَدْنَاسِ

And he should prevent him from excessive speech
For that is the habit of the blameworthy
And that he does not initiate speech
Rather his speech should be an answer

Then forbid him from swearing oaths
Always forever he should avoid them!
And from most poetry and singing
He should be prevented for all of time

Spitting, blowing his nose or expectorating
In the gathering or when someone enters
And cursing, abusing or insulting people
Mingling with people of filth

Commentary

And he should prevent him from excessive speech.

Bā Saudān says that the reason one should prohibit one's child from excessive speech is 'because excessive speech is from the attributes of crazy people.'[1] The Prophet, upon him be peace, praised silence and moderation in speech. By implication, we understand that excessive speech is blameworthy. 'Blameworthy' here means 'wicked in character' (*khabīth al-nafs*). Many of the *ḥadīth* describing the virtues of silence and moderation in speech were collected by Abu Bakr bin Abi Dunya in his book *al-Ṣumt wa Ādāb al-Lisān*. The Prophet, upon him be peace, said: 'Whoever believes in the Last Day should say good things or keep silent.'[2]

He, upon him be peace, said: 'He who keeps quiet succeeds.'[3] He, upon him be peace, also said: 'Shall I not tell you of two small things which will stand out in your meeting with Allāh—silence and good character.'[4] Excessive speech is directly contrasted with good character in the Prophetic statement: 'Surely the most beloved to me and the one who will sit closest to me on the Day of Resurrection will be the one of you who has the best character. The ones who will be the most despised by me and the ones who sit furthest from me will be those who talk excessively, do not take care about their speech and who are verbose.'[5]

And that he does not initiate speech, rather his speech should be an answer.

The child should not initiate speech unnecessarily, 'especially with someone older than him.' Rather, his speech should always be a response. This, according to Bā Saudān: 'Indicates the perfection of his intellect and respect, and the purity of his upbringing and descent.[6] The opposite indicates rashness (*ṭīsh*), triviality (*khiffa*) and haste.'[7]

Typifying the character of the Companions, may Allāh be pleased with them, 'Abdullāh bin 'Umar knew the answer to a question posed by the Prophet, upon him be peace, but did not answer as he was the youngest in the group. The Prophet, upon him be peace, asked about a tree described in the Quran as having firm roots and reaching to the sky. He knew it was a palm tree but kept silent until he got home and told his father.

Then forbid him from swearing oaths.

The child should always avoid swearing oaths by Allāh's name, whether truthful or false. Through avoiding this, he will feel the importance of Allāh's name and realise that it should not be used for worldly purposes. Allāh orders us to stay away from the one who is quick to make oaths, calling him a 'feeble oath monger'. He describes other qualities associated with this type of person:

وَلَا تُطِعْ كُلَّ حَلَّافٍ مَّهِينٍ هَمَّازٍ مَّشَّاءٍ بِنَمِيمٍ

Neither obey thou each feeble oath monger, detractor, spreader abroad of slanders. (al-Qalam 68:10–11)

He should also be prohibited from swearing oaths by anything else, even by the Kaʿba or the Prophet, upon him be peace. It has been related that: 'If one has to swear an oath, one should not swear by anything but Allāh.'[8] In some cases, the oath is not only forbidden but might also be counted as disbelief, for example, if one believes the thing being sworn by has the same status as Allāh.

And (forbid him) from most poetry and singing.

The word *al-ashʿār*, here translated as 'poetry', linguistically means 'knowledge' but in common usage and the context of this poem, it means 'speech in a metered rhythm'. What is meant by 'most poetry' is 'harmful poetry'. The principle can be traced back to the words of the Companion, ʿAbdullāh ibn ʿAmr, may Allāh be pleased with them both, who said: 'Poetry has the same status as speech. Good poetry is like good speech and ugly poetry is like ugly speech.'[9] The scholars say poetry is of two types. That which is blameworthy, which is what is meant here, and that which is beneficial, such as counsel, aphorisms and wise sayings.

Balfaqīh says the reason poetry is forbidden is so that the young person focuses on what is more important during the formative years. According to Bā Saudān, singing, *al-aghānī*, is derived from the word *al-ghinā* which is to 'use a metered voice'. Listening to it is reprehensible [whether the singer is a man or a woman], but if it leads to temptation [*fitna*], it is forbidden.[10] Among the evidences proving it is reprehensible, *makrūh*, is the statement of the Prophet, upon him be peace, that: 'Singing nourishes hypocrisy in the heart just as water nourishes vegetation.'[11]

He should be prevented from spitting, blowing his nose or expectorating in the gathering or when someone enters and cursing, abusing or insulting people and mingling with people of filth.

The last verse in this section suggests the child should be prevented from all forms of bad manners in gatherings. The author gives some specific examples of bad manners. *Al-Basq*, is something emanating from the mouth, here translated as spitting. *Al-Mukhāṭ* is that which emanates from the nose. *Al-Tanaḥḥum*, here translated as 'clearing the throat' is that which emanates from the nose but is articulated by the mouth. All are considered rude. This is even more reprehensible if the gathering includes scholars, teachers, his father or other important people.

The young person should be prevented from cursing anyone. *Li'ān* linguistically means 'to be far from Allāh's mercy.' To curse someone is the opposite of praying for them. It implies supplicating for them to be far from Allāh's mercy. Here the prohibition of cursing and other insults implies that the parent should not allow the child to become accustomed to this and other kinds of speech considered ugly by the Islamic code of behaviour.

The statement 'mingling with the people of filth' means keeping company with people who display these kinds of behaviours. Children should be kept away from people who swear, curse, spit and insult each other. The section on keeping good company deals with this principle in more detail.

Reflection

The principles and concepts expressed here are not unique or specific to Islamic culture. The association of excessive speech with fools was made by the French poet Bernard de Bonnard when he said: 'Silence is the genius of fools and one of the virtues of the wise' (*Le silence est l'esprit das sots, et l'une des vertus du sage*).[12] The phrase, attributed to Thomas Carlyle, that 'silence is golden' mirrors that of 'Abdullāh bin al-Mubārak who said 'if speech is silver, silence is gold.' Although it is unlikely that Carlyle initiated this idiom, he did make other statements in his *Essay* that 'speech is great, but silence is greater' and 'silence is more eloquent than words.'[13] These sentiments have been a part of various religious circles for centuries.Wycliffe's Bible includes the statement 'silence is made in heaven'[14] and in Rolle's *Psalms of David* that 'Disciplyne of silence is goed.'[15]

On the surface, these lines would suggest a close association with the Victorian values that 'children should be seen and not heard' and should only 'speak when spoken to.'[16] The classroom image it conjures is more like that of Mr Gradgind in *Hard Times* than the busy and apparently chaotic classrooms that I seem to be associated with. Some might say my teaching style contradicts these principles and that they are incompatible with the co-operative and active learning that I encourage. This is based on a superficial observation. I am convinced that there is no contradiction. Language, and speech in particular, is vital in learning and the transfer of culture from one generation to the next. Halliday clearly explains the connection:

> In the development of the child as a social being, language has the central role. Language is the main channel through which the patterns of living are transmitted to him, through which he learns to act as a member of a 'society'—in and through the various social groups, the family, the neighbourhood, and so on—and to adopt its 'culture', its modes of thought and action, its beliefs and its values. This does not happen by instruction, at least not in the pre-school years; nobody teaches him the principles on which social groups are organized, of their systems of beliefs, nor would he understand it if they tried. It happens indirectly, through the accumulated experience of numerous, small events, insignificant in themselves, in which his behaviour is guided and controlled, and in the course of which he contracts and develops personal relationships of all kinds. All this takes place through the medium of language.[17]

All teachers and parents 'guide and control' their children using speech. Gradgind, who sees children as 'little pitchers ... to be filled so full of facts', and the teacher encouraging active learning both have 'socialising' roles that are built on a language-power relationship. Both teachers plan their language and place restrictions on the language of the learner. My classes do not allow complete freedom to speak and once an unacceptable noise level is reached, intervention has to be swift to maintain order and continue to allow learning to take place. For me, al-Ramlī's poetry and the *ḥadīth* quoted above all point to the importance of appropriateness of language. Alice in Lewis Carroll's famous novel *Through the Looking Glass* points out the limitation of the 'speak when spoken to' principle:

> 'Speak when you're spoken to!' The Queen sharply interrupted her. 'But if everybody obeyed that rule,' said Alice, who was always ready for a little argument, 'and if you only spoke when you were spoken to, and the other person always waited for you to begin, you see nobody would ever say anything, so that –' 'Ridiculous!' cried the Queen. 'Why, don't you see, child –' here she broke off with a frown, and, after thinking for a minute, suddenly changed the subject of the conversation.[18]

I believe encouraging talk is important in the child's development. It is part of establishing *adab*. Appropriateness of social status is emphasised by the commentators when they say 'especially if the gathering includes scholars, teachers, his father or other important people.' Parents and teachers should always respect their role as teachers otherwise boundaries of *adab* will be transgressed and learning will not take place. They should be empathetic and friendly but must never forget that they are parents and teachers. Once the co-operative or active learning situation deteriorates from healthy focused discussion to the behaviour described in the poem, chaos prevails and learning ends.

The line 'his speech should be an answer' does not contradict the Vygotskian model I endorse. Vygotsky talked about a zone of proximal development which is slightly beyond what a learner can achieve without the help of a more experienced person. The teacher then 'scaffolds' the learning so that the learner develops and, after a while, is able to achieve the same thing without the 'scaffold.' In terms of language, the language of the teacher or parent needs to be targeted at this 'zone of development.' Tasks, especially language tasks, need to be set so that 'his speech should be an answer' within this zone. This is my understanding of the Prophetic advice 'to speak to people according to their ability to understand.' The meaning of *adab* here is the appropriateness of the language so that 'his speech should be an answer' to well-targeted questioning, discussion and language stimuli.

Discussion

How can young adults be encouraged to talk with their parents?

'Parents should make their children feel that they are approachable and open-minded. Although there may be barriers in age, culture and even language, if there is understanding and trust, the child will always be happy to talk to their parents.'

Taniyah Moskalyova, ESOL Teacher, Middleton

'Eating together is important. It provides routine and allows opportunities for parents to talk to their children in a fashion that is not intimidating.'

Anonymous

'Make it a point to tell your teenage children that you will always be there for them. Let them know that they can come to you with whatever concerns them. If a parent is genuinely interested in what is going on in their teenager's life, they will be receptive. Teenagers need adults that demonstrate calmness, empathy and rationality. Parents need to embody these qualities.'

Fawzia Gilani-Williams, Teacher and Author, Abu Dhabi

The Imām says 'and from most poetry and singing, he should be prohibited'. The 'metered voice' is used as a learning tool in traditional Islamic and Western education. How do parents decide which songs and rhymes are beneficial and which are harmful?

'If it is not obviously harmful, it's probably OK! There are benefits beyond religious instruction in classical poems like nursery rhymes: strengthening one's language through vocabulary, sentence construction and grammatical usage being only the most obvious of them. Believers are warned against occupying themselves too completely with poetry, such that it becomes a distraction from religious performance, the remembrance of God, or a means to disreputable environments. Again, a simple counsel in this context is the 50% rule: for every period of time one's children spend with poetry (excluding specifically religious poetry, like Qasida Burda), ensure they spend a similar amount of time with Quran or remembrance of God.'

Dr. Asim Yusuf, Consultant Psychiatrist, Walsall

Endnotes

1 Muslim, *ḥadīth* number 84.

2 Muslim, *ḥadīth* number 1726.

3 Al-Tirmidhi *ḥadīth* number 2501.

4 Ibn Abī Dunyā *ḥadīth* number 27 with a chain where all the transmitters are reliable according to al-'Irāqī.

5 Al-Tirmidhī *ḥadīth* number 2027.

6 Bā Saudān, *Simt al-'Uqyān*, 116.

7 Ibid.

8 Muslim, *ḥadīth* number 4235.

9 Muḥammad bin Isma'īl al-Bukhārī, *al-Adāb al-Mufrad* (Lahore: Makyabu Rahmāniya, no date), *ḥadīth* numbers 889, 235.

10 This is the established opinion of the Shāfi'ī School. Bā Saudān, *Simt al-'Uqyān*,120.

11 Al-Bayhaqī, *Shu'b al-Imān*, *ḥadīth* number 5100.

12 "Bernard de Bonnard," Virtue Quotes and Quotation, accessed April 10, 2010, http://thinkexist.com/quotes/withkeywords/virtue/2.html.

13 Thomas Carlyle, *On Heroes, Hero-Worship, and the Heroic in History* (Middlesex: The Echo Library, 2007), 60.

14 Book of Apocolips, Revelations (8:1).

15 Psalm CXVIII, verse 11.

16 This phrase originally referred to women and can be traced to John Mirk's *Festial* in which he says '*Hyt ys old Englysch sawe: A mayde schuld be seen, but not herd.*'

17 M.A.K. Halliday, *Language as a Social Semiotic: The Social Interpretation of Language and Meaning* (London: Edward Arnold, 1978), 9.

18 Lewis Carroll, *Through the Looking Glass and What Alice Found There* (New York: Penguin, 2001), 145.

14

GOOD MANNERS

وَيُلْزِمُوهُ كَثْرَةَ التَّوَاضُعِ - وَتَرْكَ مَا بَدَا لَهُ مِنْ طَمَعِ

وَإِنَّهُ مِنْ أَعْظَمِ الآفَاتِ - حَكَيْتُهُ نَقْلاً عَنِ الثِّقَاتِ

أَيْضاً وَمِنْ حُبِّ الذَّهَبْ وَالفِضَّةِ - يُحَذِّرُوهُ فَهْوَ أَعْظَمُ آفَةِ

مِنَ السُّمُومِ القَاتِلَهْ حُبُّهُمَا - فَالرَّأْيُ تَحْذِيرُ الصَّبِيِّ مِنْهُمَا

Make him adhere to humility
And to not covet all that appears to him
For covetousness is one of the greatest afflictions
I relate this from the trustworthy ones
And also from love of gold and silver

He should be warned against for it is an affliction
Greater than murderous poison
And as such the right judgement is to keep
The child away from them

Commentary

Make him adhere to humility and to not covet all that appears to him.

The command to 'adhere to humility' is an instruction to encourage and develop good manners. Bā Saudān says: 'Humility is the head of noble character.' The Arabic term *ḥusnul khuluq* is here translated as 'good manners' but could equally be translated as 'noble character.' *Ḥusnul khuluq*, whether translated as 'noble character' or 'good manners' is the Prophetic character. He, upon him be peace, is our role model and our aspiration when it comes to manners and character. For this reason, Allāh describes and simultaneously praises him, when He says:

وَإِنَّكَ لَعَلَى خُلُقٍ عَظِيمٍ

And thou (standest) on an exalted standard of character.
(al-Qalam 68:4)

Good character is a result of a pure relationship with the Creator. Therefore, it was the Prophets, upon all of them be peace, whose relationships involved direct revelation, who were the most noble in character. They set the 'exalted standard' for us to follow. Each of us has a portion of good character equivalent to the purity of our relationship with and adherence to the Prophetic Way and to revelation.

Al-Ḥusayn bin Manṣūr said that the meaning of 'noble character' is that 'the harshness of men does not affect you once you have become attentive to Allāh.'[1] Abū Sa'īd al-Kharrāz said 'noble character means that you have no aspiration other than Allāh, Most High.'[2] 'Abdullāh bin Muḥammad al-Rāzī remarked, 'Moral character consists of thinking little of whatever goes from you to Allāh but regarding as great whatever comes to you from Him.'[3] It is for this reason that Imām al-Ramlī mentions *tawāḍu'*, humility, specifically in this poem.

The word *tawāḍu'* comes from the root word *wa-ḍa-'a* which means to lay down or put down something, but can also have the exact opposite meaning, to erect or impose. *Tawāḍu'* is translated as humility because one lowers oneself before Allāh. Through humility before God alone, one finds true strength and power. It is for this reason that the Prophet, upon him be peace, said: 'Charity does not reduce wealth and a man who pardons only increases in status, and no one shows humility to Allāh except that he is raised.'[4] Al-Junaid said: 'Four things raise a person to the highest of ranks, even if he has only a little knowledge and a little action: forbearance, humility, generosity and good manners, and they are the perfection of faith.'[5]

Humility can best be understood through its opposite which is *kibr*, pride. Imām al-Ḥaddād said: 'From among the greatest diseases of the heart and the destroying attributes is pride. It is one of the attributes of the devils, as the Exalted said about the accursed Iblīs:'[6]

أَبَى وَاسْتَكْبَرَ وَكَانَ مِنَ الْكَافِرِينَ

He refused and was haughty: He was of those who reject Faith.
(al-Baqara 2:34)

The Messenger, upon him be peace, said: 'Allāh, the Exalted, says: "Pride is My cloak and might is My garment. I will throw whoever usurps one of them into the Fire."'[7]

'And to not covet all that appears to him' is a prohibition of *al-Tama'*, covetousness. *Al-Tama'* is defined as 'attraction of the heart to something for which one has not put forward any means of achieving it.' It is different to *al-rajā*, hope, in that hope is something that the heart is attached to (like Heaven) for which one has made some effort to achieve (such as prayer and worship). Hope is a praiseworthy characteristic and covetousness is a blameworthy one. Ibn 'Aṭāillāh said in his *Ḥikam*: 'The leaves of degradation only rise from the seeds of covetousness.'[8] What he meant by this is that once the seeds of covetousness are planted in the soul of a child, he can only grow up to live a life of degradation. We ask Allāh to protect us from this state.

I relate this from the trustworthy ones and also from love of gold and silver.

Al-Ramlī says 'I relate this to you from the trustworthy ones,' meaning those scholars whose words and actions we can depend upon. He continues by describing 'love of gold and silver', which is an 'affliction greater than murderous poison.' He bases this on the Prophet's statement when he, upon him be peace, said: 'I have left no harmful tribulation than this temporal world and women.'[9] It is also said that the temporal world is the golden calf of this nation, meaning we would make it our false god, like the Children of Israel made the calf their false god. It is that which the Prophet feared most as he said to 'Umar bin al-Khaṭṭāb who was saddened by the fact that he, upon him be peace, had temporarily decided to abstain from his wives and was lying on a coarse mat that left marks on the side of his body. He, upon him be peace, said: 'What I fear for you is that this temporal world becomes easily accessible for you and you take pleasure in it as those who enjoyed it before you, and that you are destroyed just as they were destroyed.'[10]

Among the implications of these lines, according to al-Ghāzalī, is that the parent should teach the child that giving is better than receiving and that even the poor should not sit around like dogs waiting for a morsel to be given to them. Rather, they should be taught that poverty and doing without is the characteristic of the Prophet, upon him peace, and that there is shame and disgrace in chasing after the world and no shame or disgrace in having nothing. The Prophet, upon him be peace, said: 'I sit like a slave and eat like a slave.'[11]

Reflection

When reading the classical commentaries on the topic of good character, it is clear that there is very little to add. The vast body of guidance shows the importance of the subject. Although some Muslims disagree on terminology, there is no doubt that striving to purify oneself from low and degrading characteristics is an important subject. Some call this subject Sufism or *Taṣawwuf* while others prefer the term *tazkiyatul nafs*, purification of the soul. I have no personal preference but I am worried when the use of terms becomes a sectarian issue and this is something we need to be careful about. Abū 'Abdul Raḥmān al-Sulamī said that *Taṣawwuf* used to be a reality without a name and now it is a name without a reality.

The other point that comes to mind when thinking about 'good character' is its importance in calling people to Allāh and to Islam. The Prophet, upon him be peace, said: 'I have only come to perfect good character.'[12] This implies that good character existed before him and that his role was to build on the good in people. This is vital when we are calling to Allāh and His Religion, and also in teaching young people. We should begin from a point of trying to find the good in people and not condemning them. The other important thing to note is that the Prophet's success was because of *his* good character. One can only truly call people through good character and, in particular, humility, which Bā Saudān describes as 'the head of good character.' Showing humility before children and those we are calling to Allāh or teaching is our greatest asset. We need to look after it and always strive to improve ourselves as we teach and call people.

The other attribute of good character mentioned here is detachment from the temporal world. In Arabic we call this *zuhd*. It is mentioned in the *ḥadīth* in which someone asked the Prophet, upon him be peace, about an action that would cause Allāh to love him and for people to love him. He, upon him be peace, said: 'Renounce the temporal world and Allāh will love you. Renounce what people have and they will love you.'[13] The definition of *zuhd*, renunciation, is 'turning away from something and not caring whether it comes or goes and only taking from it the amount that is required and only by legitimate means.'[14]

The problem we face in teaching our children about renunciation of the world is that they are constantly bombarded by images that are designed to attract them to the temporal world. Advertising companies have developed strategies deliberately targeted at attaching the hearts of children and young people to their products. The challenge facing parents is to guide their children away from the world without being seen as oppressive, or making their children loathe the religion. They must break the attachments that consumer society has developed.

Discussion

How do we limit the influences of mass advertising?

'We cannot limit mass advertising, but we can plant a seed that will render it redundant. That seed is to educate our children about life and good character and not how best to prepare for the rat race. Neil Postman could not have put it any better: "At its best, schooling can be about how to make a life, which is quite different from how to make a living."'[15]

Sjaad Hussain, Teacher and Researcher, Birmingham

'Most young kids see adverts as mini-programs rather than sales pitches. You have to explicitly teach young people the techniques that advertisers use to manipulate us. We also have to expose the lies they tell and show the falsehood of their claims. An example is showing them how some companies use child labour to produce clothes and the way chickens are treated to allow fast food chains to produce the junk food they sell.'

Anonymous

Endnotes

1 'Abdul Karīm al-Qushairī, *Al-Risālatul Qushairiyya fī Īlm al-Taṣawwuf* (Beirut: Dar al-Kuṭub, no date), 275–276.

2 Ibid.

3 Ibid.

4 Al-Tirmidhī, *ḥadīth* number 2097.

5 Bā Saudān, *Simt al-'Uqyān*, 125.

6 Al-Ḥaddād, *Al-Naṣāiḥ al-Dīniyya*, 362.

7 Related by Abū Dawūd *ḥadīth* number 4085.

8 *Ḥikma* number 60.

9 Al-Bukhārī *ḥadīth* number 5097 and Muslim, *ḥadīth* number 6880.

10 Related by al-Bukhārī and al-Ḥākim on the authority of Abū Huraira and classed as authentic by al-Suyūṭī.

11 Related by Aḥmad in the *Book of Zuhd*.

12 Imam Malik, *al-Muwatta*, *ḥadīth* number 2:904.

13 Ibn Mājah, *ḥadīth* number 4102.

14 Jurjānī, 291.

15 Neil Postman, *The End of Education: Redefining the Value of School* (New York: Vintage Books, 1995), x.

15

BEHAVIOUR WITH PEERS

وَيُكْرِمُ الإِخْوَانَ بِالتَّأَدُّبِ - وَكُلَّ مَنْ عَاشَرَهُ مِنْ صَاحِبِ

وَأَنْ يُوَسِّعْ لِلَّذِي يَأْتِيهِ - مَجْلِسَهُ الَّذِي اسْتَقَرَّ فِيهِ

وَيُكْرِمَ الْوَاصِلَ بِالْقِيَامِ - لأَنَّهُ مِنْ أَدَبِ الْكِرَامِ

وَيَسْتَمِعْ كَلاَمَ كُلِّ عَاقِلِ - وَيُحْسِنَ الإِصْغَا لِقَوْلِ الْقَائِلِ

لاَ يَفْتَخِرْ بِمَطْعَمٍ وَمَشْرَبِ - وَلاَ بِشَيْءٍ صَارَ مِنْ مِلْكِ الأَبِ

ثُمَّ لْيُعَظِّمْ غَايَةَ الإِعْظَامِ - مَنْ كَانَ ذَا جَاهٍ مِنَ الأَنَامِ

وَالْوَالِدَيْنِ الْكُلَّ وَالْمُؤَدِّبَا - وَالأَقْرَبِينَ نِسْبَةً وَالصَّاحِبَا

He should treat his brothers with good manners
And also those he lives with or accompanies
And he should make space for whomever
Wishes to sit in the gathering he attends

He should honour the one who enters by standing
For these are the manners of the noble ones
He should listen to the speech of every intelligent one
And lend a goodly ear to the speech of the speaker

He should not boast about his food or drink
Or any of the possessions of his father
But he should show the utmost respect
To those people of status
And parents and all the teachers
And family through lineage or marriage

Commentary

This section develops the ideas of how to behave in gatherings. It starts by mentioning that one should 'honour the believing brothers.'

He should treat his brothers with good manners.

Believing brothers are: 'Those who one accompanies in obedience of Allāh for His sake. They include his brothers and peers in his school and all companions who help him to do good or to ease his life or with whom he might travel for pilgrimage or other [beneficial trips], as well as his neighbours and other companions. He should respect the elders among them and be merciful to the younger ones. He should show gratitude for their kindness and overlook their faults. He should preserve their trusts and strive to cover up their mistakes and work hard to fulfil their needs.'[1]

And he should make space for whoever wishes to sit in the gathering he attends. He should honour the one who enters by standing.

The poet describes the *adab* of gatherings. The young person should be encouraged to make space for those who wish to attend the meeting. When someone older or knowledgeable or noble enters, he should stand and show him respect. Imām al-Nawawī says bowing the head, kissing the head, hands or feet are reprehensible, especially if the person being honoured is rich. This is based on a *ḥadīth* in which the Prophet, upon him be peace, said: 'Whoever humbles himself before a rich person, a third of his religion has gone.'[2] Others have said it is recommended to kiss the hands of scholars, nobility and one's parents based on the fact that Abu 'Ubayda kissed the hands of 'Umar bin al-Khaṭṭāb.[3]

Elders and nobility should not ask people to stand. It has been related that: 'Whoever expects people to stand for him, he has established himself a place in the Fire.'[4]

He should listen to the speech of every intelligent one and lend a goodly ear to the speech of the speaker.

The young person should listen to everyone from whom he can benefit. This is implied in the words 'every intelligent person'. Intelligence is the 'the embellishment of human nature.'[5] The young person should strive to hear, understand and benefit from every person of intellect but to stay away from arguments and people whose company leads to spite and ugliness.[6]

He should not boast about his food or drink or any of the possessions of his father.

Bā Saudān says that only those of little intellect are taken in by the superficial. They think that expensive food, clothes and the like distinguish people from one another and set some above others in rank. It is from the Prophetic tradition to hide that which one's neighbour does not have. Imām al-Ghazālī said: 'He must be forbidden to boast to his fellows about any of his parents' possessions, whether these be money or property, or anything he eats or wears, or about his tablet and pencase, and should become used to being modest, generous and mild in his speech to all with whom he associates.'[7]

But he should show the utmost respect to those people of status and parents and all the teachers and family through lineage or marriage.

The poet reiterates the importance of showing respect to elders, teachers, nobility and family.

Reflection

These *adāb*, etiquettes, of keeping company are very important. They are universal and the principles are timeless. Respecting the company you keep, making them feel welcome and listening attentively should be practised by all, regardless of culture or religion. One of the problems we face now is not only teaching these principles, but making them relevant to changing trends of socialising. Young people in Western countries socialise less as part of a family than they might do in traditional Muslim countries, or even than previous generations in the West might have done. They are less likely to see this kind of behaviour modelled. It is important that we take our children with us to gatherings from an early age so that they can see how people behave with their peers as well as their elders. We must also try to do as much as a family unit before children feel that being with their family is 'uncool'.

Discussion

How should parents deal with teenage children who don't want to participate in 'family activities'?

'This is a problem that many families face, Muslim and non-Muslim. In my experience, I find doing activities while teaming up with other families who have teenage children will help them feel it is normal to hang out with the family.'

Dr Daniel Jackson, Child Psychiatrist, Yardley

'Once they get to teenage years it is all about the activity. For example, going to the park is no longer interesting. It has to be an activity that they enjoy and that will engage them. It is not enough for them to just be with you. Instead of choosing an activity for them you should let them decide. At this stage, teenagers have already made up their minds so you need to learn to accept them for who they are and not fight them or try to mould them. It is about working with them.'

Mahmood, IT Consultant, Solihull

Endnotes

1 Bā Saudān, *Simt al-ʿUqyān*, 134.

2 Related by al-Bayhaqī on the authority of Ibn Masʿūd.

3 This refers to the occasion when 'Umar bin al-Khaṭṭāb came to Syria and is mentioned by various scholars including Ibn Ḥajar in his *Fatḥ al-Bārī* and Ibn Abī Dunya in *al-Ikhwān* and *al-Makārim*.

4 Related by al-Ṭabarānī in *al-Kabīr* on the authority of Muʿāwiya and *al-Awsaṭ* on the authority of ʿAmr bin Murra.

5 Bā Saudān, *Simt al-ʿUqyān*, 138.

6 Ibid.

7 Al-Ghazālī, *On Disciplining the Soul*, 78.

16

DISCIPLINING THE YOUNG PERSON

وَإِنْ ظَهَرْ فِعلُ الْجَمِيلِ مِنْهُ - فَيَنْبَغي بِأَنْ يُجَازَى عَنْهُ

وَأَنْ يُبَجَّلْ قَدْرُهُ وَيُمْدَحُ - بِمَا بِهِ بَيْنَ الأَنامِ يَفْرَحُ

وَإِنْ فَعَلْ فِعْلاً ذَميماً سِرًّا - فَيَنْبَغي أَنْ لاَ يُعَاقَبْ جَهْرَا

وَلاَ يُبَالِي بَعْدَهُ بِالْعَذْلِ - وَ بِالْمَلاَمِ عِنْدَ كُلِّ فِعلِ

بَلْ يَنْبَغِي عِتَابُهُ بِحَيْثُ لاَ - يَعْلَمْ عَلَيْهِ أَحَدٌ مِنَ الْمَلاَ

يَقُولُ : هَذَا – إِنْ عُلِمْ عَلَيْهِ - فَضِيحَةٌ، فَلاَ تَعُدْ إِلَيْهِ

وَلاَ تُكَثِّرْ عِنْدَهُ الْكَلاَمَا - فَإِنَّهُ يُهَوِّنُ الْمَلاَمَا

يُخْشَى بِأَنْ يَجْزِمْ وَلاَ يُبَالِي - بِمَا أَتَاهُ بَعْدُ مِنْ فِعَالِ

And if good actions from him arise
Rewarding him for that becomes necessary
His status should be raised and he should be praised
With what amongst people will bring him happiness

And if in secrecy he does a sinful act
His punishment in public should not be conducted
He should not be berated amongst all types of people
In fear that this may push him beyond his limits

Thus making him indifferent to exclusion
And to reproach to any of his actions
His reproach should be in fact
In a manner that none should know of it

He should say: if this is known about him,
It will be humiliating, so to this action do not return
Words should not be made plenty
For this will make the reproach empty

It would be feared that he becomes insistent and indifferent
To whatever actions in future he may do

Commentary

And if good actions from him arise, rewarding him for that becomes necessary.

After discussing good manners and noble character, the poet immediately refers to what the parent should do when these develop and how we should further encourage them. When these characteristics appear and the child behaves well or he shows the moral traits mentioned earlier, 'he should be praised and encouraged so that they will increase and he will strive to preserve them.'[1] Imām al-Ghazālī said: 'Whenever a good trait or action manifests itself in the child, he should be admired and rewarded with something which gives him joy, and should be praised in front of others.'[2] Balfaqīh says: 'Praise costs us nothing and has a massive effect on children.'[3]

And if in secrecy he does a sinful act, his punishment in public should not be conducted.

Bā Saudān explains what should be done if the child goes against the principles described earlier and shows bad character or does a bad act secretly. On the first occasion, you should overlook it and not expose him. The fact that the child kept it secret and made an effort to hide his action shows that he knew it was wrong. Exposing him after he has made this effort might lead him to think hiding his mistake is of no benefit and might encourage him to be bolder in his bad actions in future. If he persists and does the action a second time he should face consequences. Any punishment should be done in private and the magnitude of the action or bad trait should be drawn to his attention. You should not speak extensively or keep talking for long, as any rebuke that continues for too long leads to the child becoming accustomed to being blamed and accused. The importance and weight of the words will be lost. Imām al-Ghazālī says: 'He should not be spoken to at length every time, for this would accustom him to being blamed for his misdeeds and destroy the effectiveness such words have upon his heart. A father should rather preserve the awe in which the child holds his speech by reproaching him only sometimes. Similarly the mother, when reproving him, should frighten him [by threatening to mention the matter to his father].'[4]

Reflection

The first principle this section of the text confirms is the need for positive reinforcement. Balfaqīh's comment that 'praise costs us nothing but has a massive effect' is profound. A few years ago the importance of positive feedback was made strikingly evident. I had delivered a lecture at a university Students' Union overseas. A student in her mid-twenties approached me in the car park after the event and told me she wrote poetry. I made a very brief positive comment before getting in my car. Some years later, she told me that that comment had changed her life. She had suffered greatly in school and spent much of her teenage years in institutions due to her poor mental health and related self-esteem and eating issues. She told me that until that day, she could not remember being praised or made to feel good about her achievements. It is quite shocking how a few positive words can affect someone and how lack of encouragement can destroy someone's life and cause so much pain.

The second principle is that discipline should be in private. It is a principle I wish I knew about when I had my first encounter with discipline at a Muslim school. The pupils at that particular school were punished publicly when they misbehaved. When I challenged the proprietor of the school about the validity (and legality) of such treatment, he pointed out that the Quran mentions adulterers should be punished publicly. He drew his analogy from his understanding of these verses. I was naive and lacked the legal understanding of the Quran to respond but knew what he said was wrong. I argued my case and then went on to research the matter further. Thankfully, within a few months of being in the school, the policy was reversed and more effective, less damaging forms of discipline were introduced.

Discussion

What ways can we discipline a child?

- Withdrawing privileges
- Rewards
- Positive feedback
- Constructive criticism
- Setting clear limits
- Dialogue
- Warning

Feedback from a Workshop in Copenhagen

'There are many ways to discipline a child but the most important thing is that you are consistent and there is agreement between parents. Children need consistency and clarity and to know that they cannot play one parent against the other.'

Group of Students from Copenhagen

Endnotes

1 Bā Saudān, *Simt al-' Uqyān*, 142.

2 Al-Ghazālī, *On Disciplining the Soul*, 77.

3 Balfaqīh, *Ta'līq wa Bayān*, 102.

4 Ibid, 78.

17

AVOIDING BAD CHARACTERISTICS

يُحَذِّرُوهُ غَايَةَ التَّحْذِيرِ - مِنَ الْكَذِبْ وَالْفُحْشِ وَالْفُجُورِ

وَسَرِقَةٍ وَالأَكْلِ لِلْحَرَامِ - فَإِنَّهُ مِنْ مُوجِبِ الأَثَامِ

Extreme warnings he should be given
Of lying, illicitness and transgression

And of theft and eating from the unlawful
For it is something that leads to bad actions

Commentary

Extreme warnings he should be given of lying, illicitness and transgression.

The young person should be strongly warned against all the vices of the tongue, such as backbiting and slander. These have been discussed earlier.

Fuḥsh means to be excessive or to go over the limits and can be translated as immodest, immoderate, exorbitant, atrocity or lewdness. It includes all actions and words that are ugly. *Fujūr* means to act immorally or against the law.

And (warn him about) theft and eating from the unlawful.

After mentioning the vices of the tongue, the poet talks about the vices of the other limbs, including theft, which is a vice of the hand and eating from the prohibited, which is vice of the stomach. The young person should be warned about all vices. Aḥmed bin Zayn al-Ḥabashī explains the major vices:

- The vices of the stomach include the consumption of *ribā* (usury), drinking any intoxicant, consuming the wealth of an orphan and all foods and drinks which Allāh has made forbidden. Allāh and His Messenger, upon him be blessings and peace, cursed the drinker of wine and whoever helped him in its drinking, including the one who sold it to him.
- The vices of the tongue are numerous. They include backbiting, which is to mention something about your Muslim brother [or sister] that they would not like even if it be true, slander, lies, insults, abuse, cursing and many things besides these.
- The vices of the eye are things like looking at members of the opposite sex whom you are not allowed to look at, looking at private things [*awrāt*], looking at a Muslim with scorn and looking into someone's house without permission.
- The vices of the ear are things like listening to backbiting and other things which are prohibited.
- The vices of the hand include cheating while weighing and measuring, deceiving, stealing and all other forbidden actions such as killing or hitting someone without legitimate reason.
- The vices of the feet include going out to slander a Muslim or to kill or harm him without legitimate reason, and everything else which it is forbidden to walk to.
- The vices of the private parts are acts like *zina,*[1] sodomy,[2] masturbation and other such things.
- The vices of the whole body include unruliness towards one's parents and fleeing from the battle lines. These are considered to be from the major sins. Other things which may be mentioned besides these include cutting off family ties and abusing other people's rights.[3]

Reflection

Moral education has become an increasingly important topic of debate. Its increase stems from the perceived decline in moral standards at all levels of society, from merchant bankers to adolescents on street corners.

The thinking that has influenced much of the progressive Western tradition has its roots in the work of Jean Piaget as developed by Lawrence Kohlberg. Islamic tradition supports Piaget's observation that the child's egocentricity limits his or her moral perspective. If the child does not develop out of this state, there can be no moral development. The Islamic poet Imām al-Būṣīrī says:

> The ego is like a child: neglect it, and it will grow still suckling;
> only if you wean it, will it be weaned.[4]

Kohlberg, developing Piaget's work rejected the traditional approach to moral education and the inculcation of virtues. He identified six stages of moral development that the child needs to go through to reach a mature level of moral reasoning by which he or she can make moral and fair judgments for the good of society. Unlike the Islamic perspective, focus is on personal moral development, not on the virtue or its espousal by virtuous people. There may be something to be learned from the stages of thinking described by Kohlberg but, his basic premise contradicts Islam and traditional values which state that there are basic moral virtues which should be taught through example. All Abrahamic faiths agree on these virtues and vices.

Discussion

The sexualisation of modern day society has served to desensitise young people on issues and topics that would have been previously considered taboo. How do we deal with this when raising young adults?

'Faith schools do a good job in this respect. They talk about God and morality and take the issue head on from a young age. If we do not address this directly, children will be swamped by the images and norms and fall prey to the pressures of early sexualisation and perhaps early sexual activity. Parents have to provide an alternative view. Mosques and supplementary Muslim schools need to talk about these topics.'

Anonymous

'For me, Islamic education needs to run parallel with the education received from schools and society, so that the youth have a place to go to speak about such issues in an open and safe manner.'

Abdul Muhaymin, Medical Student, Liverpool

'Our current modern Western society over the decades has been grossly sexualised such that issues like pornography, homosexuality, open relationships, explicit clothing and so on has all become normalised and thus created a de-sensitised youth. Children brought up in an environment that is against their *fiṭra* will make them confused, and once bereft of their *fiṭra* they are then a danger to society. As parents we need to protect the early sexualisation of our children and depending on their social and personal development, teach and explain to them the matters of intimacy and relationships, as there is no shyness in religion. The environment you create around them, for example their schooling, friendship groups and home, should all help build a strong moral code within them, so when older and exposed to immorality, they will be able to make the right choices.'

Anonymous

Endnotes

1 Sexual relations with someone with whom one is not married.

2 *Lawāṭ* is anal sex with a man or woman even if she be one's wife.

3 Aḥmed bin Zayn al-Ḥabashī, *The Essentials of Islam*, trans. Abdul Aziz Ahmed (Birmingham: Islamic Village, 2008), 44–47.

4 Al-Būṣīrī, *The Mantle Adorned*, trans. Abdal Hakim Murad (London: Quilliam Press, 2008), 34.

18

ATTAINING MATURITY

فَإِنْ أَتَى وَقْتُ الْبُلُوغِ وَالصَّبِي - بِهَذِهِ الأَشْيَا خَبِيرٌ لاَ غَبِي

يُعَرِّفُوهُ مَقْصَدَ الأَشْيَاءِ - لِمُدَّةِ الدُّنْيَا وَلِلأُخْرَاءِ

وَأَنَّ كُلَّ عَيْشٍ لِلإِنْسَانِ - عَوْنٌ عَلَى عِبَادَةِ الرَّحْمَنِ

أَقْوَى لِذِي تَقْوَى عَلَى الْعِبَادَهْ - وَهْيَ الَّتِي تَحْصُلُ بِهَا السَّعَادَهْ

وَالْمَوْتُ أَقْرَبُ كُلِّ شَيْءٍ يُنْتَظَرْ - وَهَذِهِ الدُّنْيَا لَنَا دَارُ مَمَرّ

وَالآخِرَهْ دَارُ مَقَرٍّ بَاقِي - وَالآدَمِي لِفِعْلِهِ مُلاَقِي

فَيَنْبَغِي التَّكْثِيرُ لِلطَّاعَاتِ - تَزَوُّداً فِي مُدَّةِ الْحَيَاةِ

وَحِينَمَا يَنْشُو الْوَلَدْ مُؤَدَّبَا - يَكُونُ فِي بُلُوغِهِ مُهَذَّبَا

تُؤَثِّرُ الأَشْيَا بِهِ فِي الْقَلْبِ - تَأْثِيرَ حَدِّ السَّيْفِ عِنْدَ الضَّرْبِ

وَتَنْتَقِشْ فِي قَلْبِهِ مَحَبَّةْ - لِرَبِّهِ وَطَاعَةٌ وَرَغْبَةْ

لِكُلِّ مَا يُدْنِي مِنَ الْجِنَانِ - وَيَلْتَزِمْهَا دَائِمَ الزَّمَانِ

وَإِنْ وَقَعَ نَشْوُ الْوَلَدْ بِغَيْرِ مَا - قُلْنَا بِهِ ... أَضْحَى كَذُوباً نَهِمَا

مُفَاخِراً مُبَاهِياً لِلنَّاسِ - مُلاَزِماً طَبَائِعَ الْخِسَاسِ

كَلاَمَنَا لِنَفْسِهِ لاَ يَسْتَمِعْ - قَدْ صَارَ طَبْعُ لِلشَّرِّ فِيهِ مُنْطَبِعْ

And if maturity comes and the child
Of these matters is aware and not oblivious
The true purpose of things should be made known to him
And of the shortness of this life and eternity of the latter

And all worldly provision for mankind
Is an aid to him in worshipping the Most Merciful
To those with piety it will give strength in their worship
With which felicity will be attained

And death is the closest of all anticipated things
And this world for us is an abode of passage
The latter the abode of lasting residence
And the son of Adam will meet with his actions

To that end righteous deeds should be increased
In the span of life his provisions should be made
And when the child grows educated
He will be in his maturity refined

On his heart things may have an effect
Like the sharpness of a sword when it strikes
In his heart love of his Lord will be engraved
And obedience and desire

For all that brings closer to heaven
Holding tightly to it at all times
And if the upbringing of the child is contrary
To what we have said, he will become a persistent liar

Boastful and arrogant amongst people
Attached to the habits of the lowly
Our council to his self is not listened to
The habit of wretchedness on him has been imprinted

Commentary

And if maturity comes about and the child of these matters is aware and not oblivious, the true purpose of things should be known to him.

The first stage of teaching is to make the child aware of what he or she has to do and what is forbidden. This does not involve detailed explanation of the reasons, evidences and purposes of these rules. It is sufficient in the beginning to forbid the child from bad actions like stealing and swearing and to provide good role models, but once the child reaches a certain level of maturity there needs to be explanation. At this point, the young person should be taught 'the purpose of all things.' In a general sense, the purpose of life is to worship Allāh. He, the Exalted, said:

وَمَا خَلَقْتُ الْجِنَّ وَالْإِنسَ إِلَّا لِيَعْبُدُونِ

I have only created Jinns and men, that they may serve Me.
(al-Dhariyyāt 51:56)

'That they may serve Me' implies 'knowing Him' and 'worshipping Him'. The goal of establishing the good qualities mentioned earlier is that they help the young person fulfil this purpose. Guiding the child away from coloured clothes, expensive food and bad people is to focus them on their real purpose and keep them away from distractions. They should now be taught about the dangers of the world and the reasons why these distractions are harmful. They should be taught that this temporal world is short and full of obstacles that can block the way to everlasting felicity. He continues, saying the young person should be taught about the hereafter.

(He should be told about the) shortness of this life and eternity of the latter.

This life is: 'The period when man is held accountable for [responding to] the divine injunctions and prohibitions, the consequences of which will be reward or punishment, endless happiness in the proximity of God, the High and Majestic, or perpetual torment and remoteness from Him. Great individual differences exist between people as regards the length or brevity of this period, as also in other respects.'[1]

The temporal world that is this life is of three types. There is that which one lives in accordance with Allāh's commands and prohibitions; this leads to eternal felicity. There are aspects of this life that do not prevent you from fulfilling your duties nor lead you to transgression; we will be taken to account for how we indulged in these. Finally, there are aspects of this world that lead us to transgression and eternal punishment.

Our life spans may vary, with some reaching very old ages while others die as infants, but no matter how long one's life is, it has no real comparison to the eternity that follows in either the Garden or Fire. Allāh the Exalted says:

وَالْآخِرَةُ خَيْرٌ وَأَبْقَى

But the Hereafter is better and more enduring. (al-Aʿlā 87:17)

And all worldly provision for mankind is an aid to him in worshipping the Most Merciful.

This life and all it contains is a means to help us worship the Creator of life. We are expected to eat, work, marry and fulfil our duties to ourselves and others without becoming overly attached to these 'aids.' Al-Ghazālī says that if the child is brought up in the way described above, 'as he approaches adulthood he will come to understand the reasons which underlie these things, and will be told that food is a means of maintaining health and that its sole purpose is to enable man to gain strength for the worship of God [Great and Glorious is He!], and that this world is without reality, since it will not endure and that death must bring its pleasures to an end.'[2] The poem then expounds this point in the next lines:

To those with piety it will give strength in their worship with which felicity will be attained. And death is the closest of all anticipated things. And this world for us is an abode of passage—the latter abode of lasting residence.

Sa'āda is translated as 'happiness' or 'felicity'. It is 'the divine assistance granted to a person so that he or she can attain goodness. Its opposite is *shaqāwa*, wretchedness. *Musā'ada* [a word derived from the same root and usually translated as "help" or "assistance"] is assistance which we think is happiness [but actually is not].'[3]

Al-Ākhira means 'the next world' or 'the final world'. It is that which follows death. Here it refers to Heaven, which is the abode of blessing and permanent life and eternal dominion.'[4]

One of the ways that 'those with piety' gain 'strength in their worship' is by understanding the nearness of death. This leads to the shortening of 'lengthy hopes.' Imām al-Ḥaddād says:

> The meaning of lengthy hopes is 'the feeling that one will last forever in this temporal world so much so that this feeling takes over the heart and one acts accordingly.' The righteous predecessors, may Allāh show them mercy, said, 'he who extends his hopes spoils his actions.' This is because lengthy hopes lead one to covet this temporal world and make one eager to attain it, so much so that one spends day and night contemplating its acquisition and development. Considering how to attain it will sometimes be through thought and sometimes through action. One will strive for it with his exterior and in doing so, his heart and body will be immersed in it. At this point, one will forget the next world and striving for it and procrastinate in actions related to it. In his worldly matters, he will be eager and enthusiastic and in his religious duties, he will procrastinate and fall short. It should be the opposite. He should be eager about the next world which is the eternal abode and the place of permanent residence.[5]

And the son of Adam will meet with his actions. To that end righteous deeds should be increased. In the span of life his provisions should be made.

Bā Saudān says: 'Through abundant worship, faith is increased and inner sight is illumined and the heart, which is the place of Allāh's gaze, is purified.'[6] His 'span of life' is limited and he should use it as an investment in the everlasting world where he will 'meet his actions' and then enjoy his recompense.

And when the child grows educated, he will be in his maturity refined.

If the child grows up learning *adab*, he will be refined. *Muhadhab* means 'pure in character through embellishment of his character with praiseworthy qualities after removing the blameworthy ones.'[7]

On his heart things may have an effect like the sharpness of a sword when it strikes. In his heart love of his Lord will be engraved and obedience and desire. For all that which brings closer to heaven.

If 'purification' has taken place from the beginning of the child's development, he or she will have a clean heart that will be able to accept guidance. In this case, guidance and advice will be as effective as 'a sword when it strikes'. Talking about Allāh and His Messenger, upon him be peace, will lead to love and a desire to worship Allāh and follow the Messenger. Whenever he or she hears about the Garden, he or she will yearn and strive for it.

And if the upbringing of the child is contrary to what we have said, he will become a persistent liar.

If the child's upbringing is not in line with *adab*, he or she will develop bad qualities such as lying and arrogance.

Reflection

At the beginning of my teaching career, fresh out of college, I firmly subscribed to the inventionist view that adolescence is a culturally constructed concept invented at a time when it was politically and economically beneficial to create a category of people who were neither adults nor children. In part, I justified my view by the fact that in Islamic law, a child becomes an adult when the signs of puberty appear and thereafter he carries the full privileges and responsibilities of adulthood.

Joseph Kett in his *Rites of Passage*[8] shows that the concept of adolescence has varied greatly over the last two hundred years and Glen Elder's *Children of the Depression*[9] paints a very different picture of young people in America. There is no doubt that the view of young adults varies from epoch to epoch and from place to place.

As I have now seen my own children make that transition from childhood to adulthood, I have less of a socio-political interest in adolescence than a practical one. Reflecting on *The Lives of Man*, my own experiences and the reading mentioned above, I conclude that the concept of *shabābiyya*, youthfulness, is an important concept in Islam. Imām al-Ḥaddād says:

> After the onset of puberty, the first stage of youth begins, a stage where energy is abundant and strength is continually increasing, which means that it is the stage most suited for winning rewards, doing good works and avoiding reprehensible acts. However, it is also a hazardous stage of which one should be wary, for many or even most young people are inclined towards worldly desires, and prefer immediate pleasures to decent actions and observations.[10]

Even if the concept of adolescence is a socially constructed one, it is true that 'most cultures institutionalize a period of preparation for adulthood that may be analogous to adolescence as we know it. Despite some uniformities, the structure and content of the adolescent period varies markedly from culture to culture in ways that reflect broader social and institutional patterns.'[11] The real problem is that children growing up in two conflicting cultures will have different expectations placed on them. It is at this point that young people will face the most direct clash of cultures. They will be pulled by the pressure to explore an adult lifestyle prior to 'real' responsibilities, which is one cultural preparation, while Islam demands an even greater level of modesty and *adab*, which at this stage implies cultural and religious conformity. Through my personal observation of the communities I have lived in, there are serious contradictions in both generations. For many parents, it is more acceptable for a boy to experiment with the opposite sex and a Western lifestyle as long as they return to Islamic norms, than it is for girls to do the same. I have seen many young Muslim boys and girls living dual lives and facing serious internal conflicts trying to reconcile the contradictions and clashes they face on a daily basis. This situation will not repair itself. It is vital that parents and young people speak to each other and that our mosques and cultural centres start to think seriously about providing services to young people that help them grow into strong confident individuals who understand their culture, religion and the society they live in. For too long, the Muslim community has concentrated on establishing new mosques and schools without really considering this important issue.

Discussion

What pressures do young people feel growing up as Muslims in the West?

'It is hard growing up in Western culture. For me, the greatest challenges are in the way I dress and the types of relationships people have as well as music. It makes it difficult to fit in. It is a lot harder to keep in line with what your parents have taught you when you are with your non-Muslim friends. What might be acceptable for them may not be acceptable for you. I would like to adapt and integrate into that culture but I find that much of Western culture is very against our beliefs. It is very hard to keep a balance and not to lose who you are.'

Sehar Khan, School Student, Birmingham

'When it comes to culture, we are caught in between two worlds. We are neither here nor there. Nobody thinks like you. You start to make friends and then you realise how different you are and you get confused.'

Aqsa, School Student, Chryston

'One of the biggest pressures is dress. I want to wear Islamic dress but I think it draws too much attention to me. I feel more modest just blending in and not drawing attention to myself. I know hijab is important but I feel shy to wear it at school.'

Anonymous School Pupil, Copenhagen

How can parents keep the doors of communication open with young people who are growing away from the religious, cultural and family norms?

'If there is a movement away from religious and cultural norms it means that *salah*, ritual prayer, and Quran are no longer important in that household. These two elements are lifebuoys for holding onto the Rope of God. Open communication doesn't occur overnight. It's developmental. It goes from stage to stage. Children should be guided at an early age to keep company with those who do not exhibit antisocial or anti-Islamic behavior. Take an interest in who your child's friends are. Give them alternatives to what the media is constantly exposing them to. Compare how much time is spent on entertainment and how much time is spent on character development. Give importance to the message of Islam, which is in effect geared towards daily family and community problems.'

Fawzia Gilani-Williams, Teacher and Author, Abu Dhabi

'You have to start with where they are. You cannot condemn your children as it will only push them further. Sometimes you have to take an indirect approach. The priority is to get them to know that they can turn back to Allāh and talk to Him. He is Merciful and Kind and they can find comfort in talking to Him. Once there is a leaning to prayer, they will be back on the right track. Talking about secondary issues will not help, so stay away from debating what is *ḥalāl* and *ḥarām* or telling them they are heading to the hellfire. This will not help.'

Anonymous Parent, Singapore

'As long as your children have a love for the religion deep inside of them, then no matter where they go or how far they stray they will always return back to Him.'

Anonymous

Endnotes

1 'Abdullāh ibn 'Alawi al-Ḥaddād, *The Lives of Man*, trans. Dr Mostafa Badawi (London: Quilliam Press 1999), 15.

2 Al-Ghazālī, *On Disciplining the Soul*, 80.

3 Bā Saudān, *Simt al-'Uqyān*, 150.

4 Ibid, 151.

5 Al-Ḥaddād, *Taqwa and Knowledge*, 34.

6 Bā Saudān, *Simt al-'Uqyān*, 152.

7 Ibid, 153.

8 Joseph Kett, *Rites of Passage: Adolescence in America 1790 to Present* (New York: Basic Books, 1978).

9 Glen H. Jr. Elder, *Children of the Great Depression: Social change in life experience* (Chicago: University of Chicago Press, 1974).

10 Al-Ḥaddād, *The Lives of Man*, 20–21.

11 Lisa J. Crockett, "Cultural, Historical and Subcultural Contexts of Adolescence: Implications for Health and Development," *Faculty Publications* 244 (1997): 24.

19

FINAL REMARKS

فَيَنْبَغِي لِلْوَالِدِ التَّعَنِّي - بِكُلِّ مَا بِنْتٍ وَكُلِّ إِبْنِ

صَوْناً لَهُمْ عَنْ مُوجِبِ المَآثِمِ - لاَ تُهْمِلُوا الصِّبْيَانَ كَالْبَهَائِمِ

فَفِي كِتَابِ اللهِ: (قُوا أَنفُسَكُم) - مَفْهُومُهُ وَكُلَّ مَن يَلْزَمُكُمْ

أَرَادَ بِالتَّفْقِيهِ وَالتَّأْدِيبِ - وَكَثْرَةِ التَّعْلِيمِ وَالتَّهْذِيبِ

وَفِي حَدِيثٍ لِلنَّبِيِّ الْمُرْسَلِ - مُحَمَّدِ الْمُعَظَّمِ الْمُبَجَّلِ

أَنَّ الْوَلَدْ بِالْفِطْرَهْ الاسْلاَمِيَّهْ - يُولَدْ وَيَرْجِعْ بَعْدُ لِلْهُودِيَّهْ

يُهَوِّدَاهُ وَالِدَاهُ تَاعِسَا - وَقَدْ يُنَصِّرَاهُ أَوْ يُمَجِّسَا

فَإِنْ هُمَا سَاقَاهُ لِلصَّوَابِ - يُشَارِكَاهُ الْكُلُّ فِي الثَّوَابِ

فَإِنْ شَقِي وَضَاعَ مِنْ يَدَيْهِمَا - وَفَرَّطَا فَوِزْرُهُ عَلَيْهِمَا

فَهَذِهِ [رِيَاضَةُ الصِّبْيَانِ] - جَمَعْتُهَا مَنْظُومَةَ الْمَعَانِي

مُفِيدَةً لِكُلِّ مَنْ رَآهَا - وَدَبَّرَ الأَشْيَا بِمُقْتَضَاهَا

وَاللهُ يَهْدِي الْكُلَّ لِلرَّشَادِ - بِهِ اسْتَعَنْتُ فَهُوَ خَيْرُ هَادِ

ثُمَّ الصَّلَاةُ بَعْدَ حَمْدِ رَبِّي - عَلَى النَّبِيِّ الْمُصْطَفَى مِنْ كَعْبِ

وَكُلِّ آلٍ لِلنَّبِيِّ وَتَابِعِ - مَا لَاحَ بَرْقٌ فِي سَحَابٍ هَامِعِ

The parent should take care
Of every girl and boy alike
Protecting them from that which leads to bad deeds
Do not leave your children (roaming) like cattle

For in Allāh's Book it is said: Protect yourselves
It is understood and includes all within your responsibility
To mean the giving of religious knowledge and education
And increase in knowledge and refinement

And narrated from the sent Prophet Muḥammad:
That a boy in his Islamic aboriginal state
Is born and then to Judaism he may return
In the Judaic tradition they may bring him up wretchedly
Or to Christianity or Majian they may turn him

So if they guide him to the correct path
In all his good deeds they will have a share
And if he becomes wretched and from their grip he is lost
And with neglect they treated him, then his sin will be upon them

So this is Riyāḍatul Ṣibyān
I wrote it as a poem ordered in its meaning
Of benefit to all who set eye on it
And reflect on its contents and acted in accordance with it
And Allāh guides to all righteousness
From Him I seek aid for He is the best of guides

And then salutations after praise of my Lord
Upon the chosen Prophet from Kaʿb
And all the family of the Prophet and followers
With every flash of lightning that strikes a rolling cloud

Commentary

Imām al-Ramlī summarises the poem by reiterating that parents and guardians have an important responsibility to ensure that 'every girl and boy' is protected from falling into bad actions or developing bad characteristics. They should not be left like wild animals but refined and educated so they can attain felicity in both worlds. The child is naturally in a pure state and only because their environment corrupted them did they stray. The natural purity needs to be protected and developed through careful nurturing.

Bā Saudān emphasises the rights of the child over the parent: 'The right of the child over the parent is that he gives him a good name and he gets him married when he is ready and he teaches him The Book.'[1] He stresses this point by quoting various traditions on the importance of marriage, including: 'The best of my nation are those who are married' and 'Two prayer cycles from a family man is better than seventy from a single person.'[2]

The poem finishes in the traditional way, as it began with recognition that only Allāh can guide and it is upon Him that we depend. The poet then completes his prayer and advice with salutations upon the Prophet, upon him be peace.

Reflection

As I mentioned in my introduction, I am content that Allāh blessed me with children that I love and I am proud of. Before each of them were born, whilst still in the womb, Imām al-Ḥaddād's text *The Book of Assistance*[3] as well as Quran and litanies from the Prophet, upon him be peace, were read to them. As children, they were taught to read the Quran and taught the foundations of Islam as found in *The Essentials of Islam*[4] and *Hadiyatul Ikhwān*.[5] As my eldest son reached adulthood we read all three texts again and I asked him if he had been given all that he needs to live his life as a Muslim, to which he answered that he had. Although I will always be his father, the point where he said 'Yes, I have what I need' and me saying that I am content with him, was the fulfilment of our contract to each other and hopefully the fulfilment of the *amāna*, trust. I pray that Allāh protects him and his sister and the families of all that read this book and all my brothers and sisters in faith all over the world. *Āmīn*.

Endnotes

1 This is related by al-Daylamī in *Musnad al-Firdaws* and Abū Nu'aym in *al-Ḥilya* on the authority of Abū Huraira.

2 Bā Saudān, *Simt al-'Uqyān*, 159.

3 ' Abdullāh ibn 'Alawī al-Ḥaddād, *The Book of Assistance* (Louisville: Fons Vitae, 2003).

4 Al-Ḥabashī, *The Essentials of Islam*.

5 'Umar bin Aḥmed bin Sumeit, *Hadiyatul Ikhwān fi sharḥ 'Aqīdatul Imān* (Mombasa: al-Maktaba al 'Alawiyya, 1960).

GLOSSARY

Adab (Ādāb, plural)
Appropriate behaviour

Aql
Intellect

Fiqh
Jurisprudence

Fiṭra
Primordial state

Hadīth
Prophetic tradition

Ḥalāl
Permitted, sanctioned by the Islamic code

Ḥarām
Prohibited, forbidden by the Islamic code

Jumādi al-awwal
Fifth month of the Islamic lunar year

Mufti
Scholar of Islam, authorised to give binding judgements

Shaykh
Literally, 'old man', usually used to refer to an Islamic scholar

Ẓulm
Oppression or wronging of someone or something

BIBLIOGRAPHY

Ibn Athīr, *al-Nihāya fī Gharīb al-Ḥadith*. Beirut: Dar al-Iḥyah al-Turath al-Arabi, no date.

al-Aṭṭās, Sayyid Muḥammad Naqīb, *Aims and Objectives of Islamic Education*. Jeddah: Hodder and Stoughton 1977.

Balfaqīh, Ḥussain bin ʻAbdul Qādir. *Taʻlīq wa Bayān fī Sharḥ Riyāḍatul Ṣibyān*. Beirut: Dār al-Hāwi, 2002.

Bā Saudān ʻAbdullah bin Aḥmed. *Simt al- ʻUqyān*. Beirut: Dār al- Faqīh, 2004.

Baumarind, Diana. "A Blanket Injunction Disciplinary use of Spanking is not Warranted by the Date." *Paediatrics* 98 (1998): 261-267.

Baumarind, Diana. "The Discipline Controversy Revisted." *Family Relations* 45 (1996): 405-415.

Brain Gym. "Mission statement." Accessed July 15, 2010. http://www.braingym.org.

Brownhill, Simon. "The 'Brave' Man in the Early Years (0-8): The Ambiguities of being a Role Model." Paper presented to the University of Derby, Derby, January 20, 2010.

Bruce, Frederick Fyvie. "John Wycliffe and the English Bible." *Churchman*, 98/4.

al-Bukhārī, Muḥammad bin Ismaʻīl. *al-Adab al-Mufrad*. Lahore: Maktabatu Rahmāniya, no date.

al-Būṣīrī, Sharaf ad-Dīn. *The Mantle Adorned*. Translated by Abdal Hakim Murad. London: Quilliam Press, 2008.

Carlyle, Thomas. *On Heroes, Hero-Worship, and The Heroic in History*. Middlesex: The Echo Library, 2007.

Carrol, Lewis. *Through the Looking Glass and What Alice Found There*. New York: Penguin, 2001.

Crockett, Lisa J. "Cultural, Historical and Subcultural Contexts of Adolescence: Implications for Health and Development." *Faculty Publications* 244 (1997): 24.

al-Dimyāṭī, Muḥammad. *al-Jawhar al-Lu'lu'wiyya*. Damascus: Al-Yamāma, 2003.

Ibn Abī Dunya, 'Abdullāh. *al-Sumt wa Ādāb al-Lisān* in *Mawsa'āt Ibn Abī Dunya*. Beirut: Maktabatul Asriya, 2008.

"Educating Children by al-Ḥabīb 'Umar." Accessed May 9, 2009. http://daralmustafaedu.com/.

Elder, Glen H., Jr. *Children of the Great Depression: Social change in life experience*. Chicago, IL: University of Chicago Press, 1974.

Food Research and Action Center. "School Breakfast Program." Accessed March 19, 2013. http://frac.org/wp-content/uploads/2009/09/school_breakfast_program_fact_sheetpdf.

Gershoff, Elizabeth Thompson. "Corporal Punishment by Parents and Associated Child Behaviours and Experiences: A meta-Analytic and Theoretical Review." *Psychological Bulletin* 128 (2002): 539-579.

al-Ghazālī, Muḥammad. *Al-Ghazālī On Disciplining the Soul and Breaking the Two Desires with an introduction and notes*. Translated by T. J. Winter. Cambridge: Islamic Texts Society, 2001.

al-Ghazālī, Muḥammad. *Al-Ghazālī on The Manners Relating to Eating*. Translated by D. Johnson-Davies. Cambridge: The Islamic Texts Society, 2000.

al-Ḥabashī, Aḥmed bin Zayn. *The Essentials of Islam*. Translated by Abdul Aziz Ahmed. Birmingham: Islamic Village, 2008.

al-Ḥaddād, 'Abdullāh bin 'Alawi. *al-Nasāiḥ al-Dīnniyya wal Waṣāyā al-Imāniyya*. Beirut: Dar al-Hāwi, 1999.

al-Ḥaddād, 'Abdullāh bin 'Alawi. *Taqwa and Knowledge*. Translated by Abdul Aziz Ahmed. Glasgow: Islamic Texts for the Blind, 2010.

al-Ḥaddād 'Abdullāh bin 'Alawi. *The Lives of Man*. Translated by Dr Mostafa Badawi. London: Quilliam Press, 1991.

al-Ḥaddād, ʿAlawi bin Ṭāhir. *ʿUqūd al-Almās bi Manāqib al-Ḥabīb Aḥmed bin Ḥasan al-ʿAṭṭās*. Singapore: Karaji Press, 1991.

Halliday, M. A. K. *Language as Social Semiotic: The social interpretation of Language and Meaning*. London: Edward Arnold, 1978.

Horten, M. *Die Philosophie des Islamin ihren Beziehungen sudden philosophischen Weltanschauungen des westlichen Orients*. Munich: 1924.

Howard, Barbara J. "Guidance for Effective Discipline." *Paediatrics* 101 (1998): 723- 728.

al-Jawziyya, Ibn Qayyim. *Medicine of the Prophet*. Translated by Penelope Johnstone. Cambridge: Islamic Texts Society, 1998.

Kett, Joseph. *Rites of Passage: Adolescence in America, 1790 to Present*. New York: Basic Books, 1978.

Nairn, Agnes. *Child Well-being in the UK, Spain and Sweden: The Role of Inequality and Materialism*. London: Ipsos-MORI Social Research Institute, 2011.

al-Nawawī, Abu Zakaria Mohiuddin Yahya bin Sharaf. *Etiquette with the Quran*. Translated by Musa Furber. Berkeley: Starlatch Press, 2003.

Palmer, Sue. *Detoxing Childhood: What parents need to know to raise happy and successful children*. London: Orion Books, 2007.

al-Qushairī, ʿAbdul Karīm. *al-Risālatul Qushairiyya fī ʿIlm al-Taṣawwuf*. Beirut: Dar al-Kuṭub, no date.

al-Qurṭubi, Abu ʿAbdullāh Muhammad Aḥmed al-Ansari. *Anwār al-Tanzīl wa Asrār al-Tawīl*. Beirut: Dar al-Kuṭub, 1988.

al-Ramlī, Muḥammad bin Aḥmed. *Fawāid al-Mardiyya: Sharḥ Mukhtaṣar al-Muqadimatul Ḥarḍrāmiyya*. Jeddah: Alam al-Maʿrūf, 1999.

Rousseau, Jean-Jacques. *Emile*. Vermont: Everyman, 1993.

Rolle, Richard. *The English Writings*. Edited and translated by Rosamund S. Allen. New York: The Paulist Press, 1976.

Schor, Juliet B. *Born to Buy*. New York: Scribner, 2004.

bin Sumeit, ʿUmar bin Aḥmed. *Hadiyatul Ikhwān fi Sharḥ ʿAqīdatul Imān: a short treatise on the principles of faith*. Mombasa: al-Maktaba al-ʿAlawiya, 1960.

Virtue Quotes and Quotation. "Bernard de Bonnard." Accessed April 10, 2010.

http://thinkexist.com/quotes/withkeywords/virtues/2.html.

Vygotsky, L.S. *Mind in Society: Development of Higher Psychological Processes.* Cambridge: Harvard University Press, 1978.

Words Spy. "Busy Brain." Accessed July 15, 2010. http://www.wordspy.com/words/busybrain.asp.

PEOPLE MENTIONED IN THE TEST

ʿAbdullāh bin al-Mubārak
Ascetic scholar of Khorasan died 181 H, 797 CE.

ibn Abī Dunya, ʿAbdullāh
Ḥadīth scholar, died in 281 H.

al-Anṣāri, Zakariyya
15th Century Egyptian scholar, died 1520 CE.

Asad, Muḥammad
Austrian scholar and diplomat, author of Road to Mecca, *known as Leopold Weis and died 1992.*

ibn ʿAṭāillāh al-Iskandarī
Mālikī scholar and mystic of the Shadhilī order, died 1309 CE.

Aḥmed Bin al-Mubārak
Moroccan mystic died 1743 CE.

al-ʿAṭṭas, Sayyid Muḥammad Naqīb
Contemporary Malaysian philosopher and scholar, born 1931 CE.

al-ʿAṭṭās, Ṣāliḥ bin ʿAbdullāh
Ḥadrāmī scholar died 1289 H, 1872 CE.

al-Baghawī, Imām
Persian commentator on Quran, ḥadīth scholar and jurist, died 516 H, 1122 CE.

de Bonnard, Bernard
French poet, died 1784 CE.

al-Būṣīrī, Imām
Poet and mystic, author of the acclaimed Burda, died 696 H, 1294 CE.

Bin Sumait , 'Umar bin Zayn
Ḥadrāmī scholar died 1207 H, 1792 CE.

Carlyle, Thomas
Scottish satirical writer, died 1881.

Carroll, Lewis
English author, mathematician, Anglican Deacon, died 1898.

Dennison, Paul
Educationalist, founder of the Kinesiology Foundation and developer of the Braingym programme.

Dewey, John
American philosopher, psychologist and educationalist, died 1952 CE.

al-Dāraquṭnī, Imām
Ḥadīth scholar, died 385 H, 995 CE.

Elder, Glen
American sociologist, born 1934.

al-Ghazālī, Imām Muḥammad
Scholar and author of the famous Ihyā Ulūm al-Dīn, *died 505 H, 1111 CE.*

al-Ḥabashī, Aidarūs bin 'Umar
Ḥadrāmī scholar and historian died 1314 H, 1896 CE.

al-Ḥabashī, Aḥmed bin Zayn
Ḥadrāmī Scholar, student of Imām al-Ḥaddād and commentator on his works, died 1145 H, 1732 CE.

al-Ḥaddād, Imām 'Abdullāh bin 'Alawī
Scholar and spiritual master, author of many books some of which have been translated into English, died 1132 H, 1720 CE.

al-Ḥaddād, Aḥmed bin Ḥasan bin 'Abdullāh
Grandson of Imām al-Ḥaddād, died 1204 H, 1790 CE.

al-Ḥaddād, Aḥmed Mashūr
Twentieth century scholar and caller to Islam, died 1418 H, 1997.

al-ḥaddad Ṭāhir bin ʿUmar
Hadrami scholar died 1319 H, 1901 CE.

Ibn Ḥajar, Imām
Egyptian jurist and ḥadīth scholar, died 852 H, 1449 CE.

al-Husayn bin Manṣūr
Persian mystic, died 309 H, 922 CE.

Halliday, Michael
English Linguist born in 1925.

al-ʿIrāqī, Zaynuddīn
Ḥadith scholar born in Iraq 725H, 1325CE, died in Egypt 806 H, 1404 CE.

al-Junaid, Abū Qāsim
Scholar who combined the mystical and legal codes of Islam, died 367 H, 977 CE.

Kett, Joseph
Professor of American Intellectual Cultural History at University of Virginia.

al-Kharrāz, Abū Saʿīd
Early mystic of Baghdad believed to have died around 280 H, 893 CE.

al-Khitamy, Abdul Raḥmān
Kenyan scholar and herbalist, died 1426 H, 2005 CE.

al-Mālikī, Muḥammad bin ʿAlawī
Ḥadīth scholar of Makka, died 1424 H, 2004 CE.

Montessori, Maria
Italian educator who influenced modern thinking on child development, died 1952.

al-Munawī, ʿAbdul Raūf
Egyptian ḥadīth scholar, died 1031 H, 1621 CE.

Ibn Qayyim al-Jawziyya
Jurist and theologian, died 751 H, 1350 CE.

Kohlberg, Lawrence
American psychologist and academic who wrote on moral education, died 1987.

al-Nawawī, Imām
Ascetic ḥadīth scholar and jurist, died 676 H, 1277 CE.

Palmer, Sue
Former Headteacher and writer on parenting, born in Manchester 1948.

Piaget, Jean
Swiss developmental psychologist, famous for his theory of cognitive development, died 1980.

al-Qurṭubī, Imām
Andalusian Jurist and Quran exegete, died 671 H, 1273 CE.

Rousseau, Jean-Jacques
Genevan philosopher and author of Emile and other books which influenced the French Romantic movement, died 1778.

al-Shaʿrānī, ʿAbdul Wahāb
Ascetic scholar of jurisprudence, ḥadīth and Quran, died in Cairo in 973 H, 1565 CE.

Schor, Juliet
American Professor of sociology and writer, her studies include relationship between work and family.

Rolle, Richard of Hampole
Hermit and translator of the Bible, 1290–1349 CE.

Ṭāhir bin Ḥussain bin Tāhir
Ḥadrāmī scholar died 1241 H, 1825 CE.

Vygotsky, Lev
Russian psychologist, died 1934.

Wycliffe, John
English theologian and Bible translator, died 1384.

Printed in the USA
CPSIA information can be obtained
at www.ICGtesting.com
LVHW040802210923
758364LV00003B/13

9 781915 025890